Turin

portrait of a city

Luigi Firpo

TURIN

portrait
of a city

TIPOGRAFIA TORINESE EDITRICE

140 pages
185 engravings and photographs
20 illustrations in colour

Original title

TORINO, RITRATTO DI UNA CITTÀ

English translation by
A. Ernest Howell

CONVENTIONAL TOURIST ROUTES ignore Turin. There are, in fact, no flowering orange trees as at Taormina, or roses as at Paestum; there are not the magnificent Greek temples of Agrigento, the Coliseum and basilicas of Rome, or the Byzantine mosaics of Ravenna. No Ruskin has idealised its ancient stones or its cold mornings; its University has never attracted the foreign students who once flocked in thousands to Padua or Bologna; no scion of the nobility from beyond the Alps ever honoured it with a stay in the obligatory Grand Tour which brought him to Italy to learn fencing and dancing, riding and gallantry.

In the golden age of Italian civilisation that was the Renaissance, when Naples numbered three hundred thousand inhabitants and Milan and Venice each one hundred and fifty, Turin was little more than a village. It later became the capital of a poor and mountainous small state, ravaged by continual wars, overrun and pillaged by all the armies of Europe, and much more inclined to breed bureaucrats and soldiers than art patrons and artists. It was slow in attaining the rank of a real city and underwent a feverish growth only in the age of the industrial revolution which covered many ancient settlements with the sores of urbanisation, with smoky and dreary factories and densely populated tenements; the second world war brought to it fire and destruction; and later at least half a million poor people, escaping from a depressed countryside, arrived from all sides to seek work, a home and a future for their children.

This is true, but anyone who expects to visit a hive of factories and swarming humanity, an anonymous expanse of concrete and glass, must undeceive himself. Turin is one of the most harmonious and clearly planned cities that exist; it is the result of an ever renewed cartesian will, that seems to spread out concentrically from age to age, to reduce the arbitrary, the chaotic and the shapeless to models of pure reason. In Turin at least four towns survive, one inside the other like Chinese boxes, four moments of clearly defined renewal, where the later does not repudiate the earlier but on the contrary projects it into a new dimension, preserving intact the spirit that informs it. This spirit — inflexible will, functional geometry, flashes of repressed inspiration — is expressed in the collective, coordinated and uniform character of the urban texture, in a state of continuous tension against anarchical individualism and capricious variation. These four towns are: Roman Turin (structurally intact down to the beginning of the 17th century), baroque Turin, Turin of the Risorgimento and Turin of the motor car.

The first three, which more or less constitute the « historic centre », present, over a relatively small area, a very dense concentration of notable buildings, of museums filled with masterpieces, of historical memories and monuments, which together form a whole of unique quality and compactness.

Fantastic pinnacles soar above the highest peaks of the Turinese hills, from which the eye ranges over the city and the circle of the Alps.

The Beacon of Victory on the summit of the Maddalena hill commemorates the fallen of the First World War. The enormous, dramatic bronze figure is by Edoardo Rubino (1928).

The elaborate, curving belfry designed by Filippo Juvarra (1716) for the campanile of the basilica of Superga.

opposite page:

Plan of the Roman city drawn by Alfredo d'Andrade (Turin, Civic Museum of Ancient Art). The walls ran, to the east between the present Via Roma and Via Lagrange, to the south along Via S. Teresa, to the west along Via della Consolata, while to the north they were aligned with the surviving Palatine Gate.

Bronze bull from the excavations at Industria and a fragment of bas-relief representing a Roman legionary (Turin, Museum of Antiquities).

Here there is nothing of the opulent variety, the mingling of periods, styles and dominations that other cities reveal at first glance: on the contrary, it is as if the new sprang from the old, harmonised with it quietly and without jarring, immediately taking on a patina and local colour, as if everything — the layout of the streets, the buildings, churches, trees, monuments — blended together to express the compact unity of a civilisation. For this, too, must be said: that other cities express — and sometimes in an astonishing way — one or more cultures, but in Turin one breathes above all a way of existence and of understanding life: brusque and yet friendly, reserved but not haughty, witty but not sarcastic. The city conceals a quiet patience, a cautious but not boastful optimism, a persistent search for clarity. Respect for decorum, a quiet strength, a very rare and usually hidden showiness, are but the architectural equivalent of the Piedmontese character, tendentially egalitarian, conscious of the dignity of civil and common duties accepted with dedication and pride, that is in both a religious and military spirit.

This uniformity without monotony, this absence of strident notes, have induced some to speak of Turin as of a dull and commonplace city, lacking in works of art, while it is in fact — as one of its writers, Augusto Monti, has shrewdly defined it — a *fausse maigre*, its beauty modest and coy, but brimming over with hidden charms. To know Turin, therefore, to prepare oneself to love it, requires a certain effort, an ability to hear the voices of time and to interpret their secret message.

One then discovers that the urban scene, at first sight monochrome and repetitive, is in reality a subtle counterpoint — an amalgam which the centuries have overlaid with a patina of disparate historical evidences and which the changing seasons imbue with ever new delights. The stark images of the technological age, with its obsessive forms, its shining metal towers and symmetrical labyrinths, thus alternate with survivals from a provincial past: quiet squares, long grey streets closed by the white backdrop of distant peaks, damp autumn parks with a carpet of red leaves, a pale sun shining

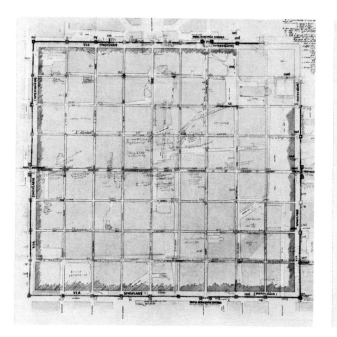

on patches of fresh snow and dispersing the light mist, windy spring days which make the air like glass and the mountains seem so near that you can almost touch them, thick fogs at dusk which deaden the sounds and inspire joyful bursts of energy.

Perhaps the best way to try and understand the city is to study it from above and from a distance. One must go outside it and climb to the top of one of the highest hills — Superga or the Maddalena — after a day of wind. The surrounding hills, no one like the other, all little knolls and valleys, studded with villas, fields and dark woods, stand like the centre of an immense wheel, like a wedge which presses the great loop of the Po to the nearby mountains. From north to south, over all the western arc, the mountains rise compact and shining, one above the other and formed by the perspective into a single range : to the left the Monviso raises its sharp pyramid, to the right the Monte Rosa reflects a suffused light from its timeless glaciers. And the view stretches even farther, from the Maritime to the Lombard Alps, revealing in its entirety what was for centuries the real, the little Piedmont: not the historical region which political astuteness and warlike valour welded together in the 18th century, but the much more restricted geographical region of the « flat country at the foot of the mountains » — this half-circle of alluvial land between the Tanaro and the Sesia, furrowed by a hundred torrents, gravelly, well-watered, poor, more suited to woods than to crops, but tamed and sweetened by two thousand years of human toil.

At the very centre of the arc, where the Po laps the foot of the hills and the gap between the river and the mountains becomes narrower, at the mouth of the easiest of the western Alpine passes, Ligurian peoples founded Turin, an obligatory place of passage, well protected on a steep terrace of land, at the confluence of the Dora and the Po. An uncouth people, tempered by dour adversities (Virgil calls them hardened to suffering: « adsuetumque malo Ligurem ») and certainly mixed

The most illustrious graduate of Turin University: Erasmus of Rotterdam in an anonymous woodcut of 1521 reproduced on the front of a small book by Hans Eberling.

opposite page:
Very little survives of the rustic Turin of the late Middles Ages and early 16th century.

The Medieval Village in the Valentino is a nineteenth century reconstruction, but offers a vivid and colourful picture of a Piedmontese village of the 15th century.

Medieval mullioned window framed by a terracotta frieze.

Flat-topped window of a 16th century house in Via IV Marzo.

Door-jambs and pilaster strips of the Cathedral carved around 1500 by the Tuscans Meo del Caprina and Sandrino di Giovanni.

with Celtic stock, bringing their native character of patient stubbornness, sudden irrational bursts of temper and cheerful craziness. One still finds in the Aosta and Susa valleys some of these almost pure Celts — little men with round heads and drooping moustaches, and a rather haunted look in their eyes like that you see in wild goats. The first « Taurini » were certainly tillers of the soil and growers of crops, and it does not matter if the spirited young bronze bulls dug up not far away at Industria were not symbols of an archaic bucolic civilisation but later votive offerings of an Isiac cult. With these characteristics of harsh obstinacy and sudden madness Turin enters history for the first time in the September of 218 B. C.: Hannibal's vast army of widely differing peoples and customs, with their frightful elephants, weapons and machines of war, crosses the Mont Cenis pass and spreads out over the plain. Resistance is impossible. But Turin does not open its gates, it fights stubbornly, and after three days is razed to the ground and exterminated down to the last man.

With no less harshness it was rebuilt by Rome as the colony of Augusta with a few thousand veterans: people of various Italic lands grown old under the standards, tempered by many privations. They came here already white-haired, beating their swords into ploughshares to till the fields, and the inscriptions speak of veterans' associations to celebrate convivial anniversaries and funeral ceremonies: one seems to hear again the gurgling of wine in the rustic cups, the hoarse voices, the stories of sieges and battles in the forests of the North and the fabulous East. It was they who laid out the city as a *castrum*, with its network of right-angled streets, its square walls, its four gates: and in that form, on that small plot of ground — the whole perimeter measured less than three kilometres — Turin lived century after century, almost unchanged.

The remains of a small theatre, the two towers of the Decuman gate incorporated in Palazzo Madama, the bare and solemn Palatine gate with its solid tawny masonry, a fragment of wall and some broken statues are all that is left of the colony of *Julia Augusta Taurinorum*; but the narrow alleys of the old centre still faithfully follow its plan, their blackened fronts, the damp well-shafts of their courtyards and their lightless shops huddled together along the lines traced by the legionaries.

History began to flow like a slow, dark river. Sarmatians and Goths, Burgundians and Lombards, Hungarians and Saracens passed; the descendants of Arduino, Angevins, the Houses of Savoy and Acaia, bishops and marquises ruled; but little or nothing changed in the big walled village packed with artisans' shops, warehouses, taverns and stables. It was a staging-point, a place of passage, overcrowded, noisy, swarming with common people, without a notable building, without a work of art, without ambitions and examples of a more refined life, cultured amusements or courtly luxury. There were few professional men, very few nobles in that small middle-

class centre of craftsmen and merchants far from the mainstream of culture; and yet the people who went their ways in it were affable and jocular, without refinement but ennobled by a natural courtesy, that spontaneous *humanitas* that so struck Erasmus when he came to take his degree at Turin in 1506.

It is almost impossible, after so much and such radical rebuilding, to reconstruct the appearance of the town in the fifteenth and sixteenth centuries, with its low plastered houses overhanging the narrow streets with their projecting roofs, wooden galleries, mouldings and windows decorated with terracotta friezes and brightly coloured frescoes, the streets themselves lined by low pointed-arched arcades with pillars supporting each other to buttress them, so welcome when the sleet is whirling. And in the streets there was the gaily-coloured throng, brisk and lively, with the sparkle of their Gallo-Roman speech rich in proverbs, ingenious metaphors and witty sayings. The scene was that of the streets today in one of the old villages such as Cavallermaggiore or Cirié, with the country reaching to their very centre, with the smells of hay and wood, of grain and must, of forge and stable. Only a few pathetic fragments of this tawny village by the Po — some mullioned or fine flat-topped window — still catch the eye in the oldest part of the town, between the Cathedral and the City Hall, like survivors from an irreclaimable shipwreck. Then there is the badly tampered with church of St. Dominic, of Lombard-Gothic inspiration, with its pointed portal of ornamental brick, and the towers and halls of Ludovico d'Acaia, who transformed Palazzo Madama in the early fifteenth century. Scanty, too, are the evidences of the Renaissance: the Cathedral dedicated to the Baptist, which Meo del Caprina began in 1491, translating with frigid correctness the Tuscan models of Brunelleschi and Alberti, which stand out like something exotic under the Supalpine sky, and the slender grace of the courtyard of the Scaglia di Verrua palace in Via Stampatori.

La Pianta de Turino.

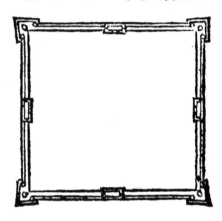

The earliest surviving picture of Turin, the first of a long series, saw the light in 1538 in the small work of a Milanese poetaster, an easy target for the shafts of Aretino: the *Istoria della guerra di Piamonte* by Giovanni Alberto Albicante. It gives a completely imaginary view of the town in the form of a turreted fortress, with megalithic walls bristling with cannon — the almost symbolic anticipation of an austere and warlike vocation, which was to mature in the centuries to come. Even more fanciful is the Turin depicted in 1552 by Sebastiano Münster, which becomes decidedly improbable, surmounted as it is by gothic cusps and bordering a river so incredibly abounding in fish as to be actually swarming with lobsters. This means only that Turin was in reality a town without any character, a geographical expression.

Among the imaginary views may be placed the plan drawn in 1546 with mathematical exactness by Niccoló Tartaglia, who leaves out the buildings but renders almost perfectly the four massive walls of the *castrum* protected at the corners by the bulges of as many projecting bastions. These had been erected ten years before, in great haste, by the good Duke Charles II, to defend himself against the advancing French; but he had realised in time that the town was not defensible and had evacuated it on 27 March 1536, taking with him a few possessions, a handful of loyal supporters and a child of eight, who soon learnt the lesson that the weak are always wrong. For more than a quarter of a century after this Turin became a French city. Guillaume De Bellay was installed as Governor of Piedmont and his personal physician wrote a book of warlike stories and begot an illegitimate child there, besides giving the final touches to his masterpiece: *Gargantua and Pantagruel*. At Turin in 1544 died that charming poet Clément Marot and in 1548 Henri II made his solemn entrance, as if to give official sanction to possession of the new province. In a Piedmont depopulated and sacked by Spaniards and French the people lost all interest in work and only thought of having as good a time as they could. Giulio Cesare Scagliero wrote that the Piedmontese at that time led a carefree life, liking nothing but dancing, and the Venetian ambassadors spread the saying round Europe: « Piemontese e Monferrin — pane, vino e tamburin », which has nothing festive about it as it always wrings the heart to see people drinking and singing to forget their misfortunes. However that may be, it is too soon to expect to find an austere Piedmontese, all home and duty, in the later sixteenth and early seventeenth century: if to eat, drink and dance is the ideal of this rather foul-mouthed and coarse society, it is because the people are accustomed to taking life philosophically, to rolling up their sleeves after each pillage or flood, and to seeking, after the job is done, a little noisy and carefree amusement.

But not everything goes to rack and ruin. While Vercelli and Cuneo hold out unbeaten, Turin works; it was in fact a Venetian, Minucci, visiting it in 1549, who described it as

The oldest graphic representations of the city:

The first imaginary view of Turin: wood-engraving from G. A. Albicante's « Istoria de la guerra del Piemonte », Milan, 1538.

Another imaginary view of Turin in the « Cosmographia universalis » by Sebastian Münster, printed at Basle in 1552.

Plan of the fortifications of Turin in 1546 (from the « Quesiti » by Niccolò Tartaglia, printed in that year at Venice).

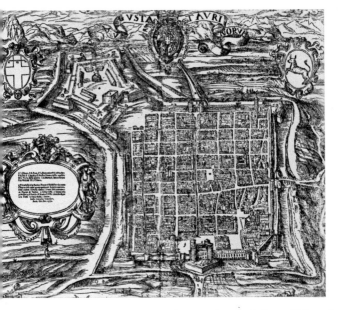

small, populous, rich, solid and — an extraordinary adjective for a commercial town — silent. Why did the chatter of the Rialto not resound in our market square at the foot of the pointed civic tower? A dash of intractable Subalpine reserve emerges from the page, showing that the ancient character was firmly rooted.

On 7 February 1563 the town was *en fête*. The boy exile, now the victor of St. Quentin and restorer of the state, was re-entering it justifiably proud and elated. Piedmont had more populous towns, such as Mondovì and Chieri, better defended fortresses, centres richer in illustrious traditions: but Turin was at the heart of the Italian dominions of the House of Savoy, lying as it did between Aosta and Oneglia, between Ivrea and Asti, at the mouth of the Susa Valley, the natural gate to their lands beyond the Alps. So Emmanuel Philibert fixed the permanent capital of his states here, transferring the university from Mondovì, the Senate from Carignano, and the Holy Shroud from Chambéry. The town did not even have a decent residence to offer the Duke, but he did without it, went to live in the Bishop's decrepit house and employed bricks and money to erect, instead of a luxurious dwelling, the austere pentagon-shaped Citadel, the marvel of military engineering of the time and bulwark of regained liberty. For in May 1564, a little over a year after his re-entry, the Duke was calling for bids to build the fortress — of which to-day only the square keep survives.

Francesco Paciotto designed it according to the most up to date ideas, with squat terreplein ramparts and a star-shaped plan, which allowed all the curtain-walls to be swept with fire. The hastily erected stronghold, with absolute priority over any other building, was the sign that the hard lesson of childhood had been learnt to the full and was at the same time a massive symbol of Turin's future destiny.

In its new square shape, crowded with huts, pointed ramparts, turreted gates and, high up, the fortified pentagon of the fortress — which the Duke called « the most precious jewel in his treasury » — the town leaves the realms of

Culture and court life at the beginning of the 17th century: the original edition of the « Primavera » of Giovanni Botero printed at Turin in 1607.

Turin spreads beyond its Roman boundaries: view of the town in 1633, showing the progress of the works for the first expansion towards Porta Nuova. Engraving by Giovenale Boetto.

Plan of Turin in 1640, at the time of the siege. Detail of an engraving by Boetto.

fantasy and enters history, thanks to the excellent map which Johann Criegher engraved on wood in 1572 to the design of Carracha, a Fleming. In the civic coat of arms a young, unhaltered but not yet rampant bull seems to scamper over green fields beside the Dora. To call it a town is nevertheless an exaggeration: it had about 14,000 inhabitants when Michel de Montaigne, on his way home after his grand tour of Italy, passed through it in a hurry on 30 October 1581 and described it as a « small town on a very watery site, not very well built or pleasant, with, moreover, a stream running down the middle of the streets to carry away the filth ». Its growth was slow, almost laborious, and the plague of 1599 retarded its demographic development, so that the inhabitants were barely 16,000 in 1601, some 20,000 three years later, and 30,000 in 1630, when a new pestilence, reaping 3,000 victims and putting the survivors to flight, depopulated it again. Its ancient rural, village-like appearance, too, was slow to disappear: it was only in 1602 that the streets began to be paved and the Castle Square levelled where, in the following decade, the first arcaded buildings were to rise; only in 1620 was the New Gate breached in the old walls, on the axis of a straightened street that was to become the first section of the present Via Roma. Nothing yet impressed the visitors, who speak only of the solid fortress, the deep moats and the abundant artillery.

Even a sacred ceremony like the exhibition of the Holy Shroud in 1613, delineated in masterly fashion by Antonio Tempesta, bristles with halberds and is packed with soldiers firing salvoes; while to have a better view a curious spectator has even climbed onto a cannon. In 1618 a Venetian ambassador said that Turin was « a small town, but very populous and in an agreeable and very beautiful spot », enclosed in its ancient square of walls and crowded with workmen, shopkeepers and busy artisans. The social fabric was still middle-class and plebeian; the nobility still lived far away in their old castles and the court, uncomfortably housed in the chaotic and evil-smelling buildings inside the town, sought escape in

the pleasant villas nearby. Admiring the splendid country seats dear to the French, the Subalpine élite set up its own imitations of Versailles, surrounding Turin with a ring of castles, parks and villas for its relaxation. So there came into being between one war and another Mirafiori and Mille-fonti, Rivoli, and Moncalieri, Venaria and Regio Parco, Mada-ma Reale's « Vineyard » and the Queen's Villa; while nearer the walls, on the gentle bend in the Po, the Queen Regent com-pleted the Valentino Castle. This was in 1660. On its delight-ful gardens the poets of Italy — Tasso and Guarini, Tassoni and Testi, Marino and Chiabrera — seemed to gather, exiles in a rustic Boeotia; even the venerable Botero gave up political theory to write the harmonious, if rather senile, octaves of his *Primavera*.

Meanwhile the town was growing, and for the first time burst its banks. To the south Carlo di Castellamonte laid out the quarter of Porta Nuova, but prudently, before erecting any buildings, the area was first girt with massive ramparts. A charmingly fresh view by Giovenale Boetto (1633) just catches the excitement of the plans and work: in one corner the famous engraver from Fossano skilfully includes a lively portrait of himself when young that is worthy of Romijn de Hooghe. It was Boetto who, the year after, delineated for us the oath by the League of the Catholic Cantons, including an extraordinary number of characters under the austere arches of the cathedral; and he again who in 1638 perpetuated Victor Amadeus's solemn funeral procession — a triumph of violent Baroque in a composition whimsically filled out with skele-tons and images, trumpets and torches, coats of arms and scrolls, all immersed in a dark sepulchral light.

It was only in 1650 that the first frivolous views appeared, such as the tournament proclaimed by the sixteen-year-old Charles Emmanuel II or the church of St. Salvario in open country as the background to a hunting party galloping under the leafy boughs of ancient trees. At this point even the big village that had been a captial now for more than a century,

Amusements of seventeenth century society: the gathering for a hunt near the small surburban church of S. Salvario, in the modern Via Nizza, designed by Amedeo di Castellamonte in 1646. Engraving by Giovenale Boetto (about 1650).

Victor Amadeus II, not yet ten years old, on a prancing horse in front of the Military Academy, designed by Amedeo di Castellamonte and completed in 1677. Copper engraving of Antonio de Pienne.

Niche in the façade of Palazzo Carignano begun by Guarini in 1679.

Art and culture at the service of princely pomp: frontispiece of Guarino Guarini's « Disegni » (Turin, 1686).

opposite page:

Plan and symbols of the town and the Po engraved by Giorgio Tasnière for the fly-leaf of the « Historia dell'augusta città di Torino » of Emanuele Tesauro (Turin, 1679).

The French edition, issued at the Hague in 1700, of the sumptuous collection of views of the « Theatrum Sabaudiae » published for the first time at Amsterdam in 1682.

sloughed its skin, seized, it seemed, with a fever of total renewal. It set out to pull down the squalid hovels and erect stately buildings in their place. In a few decades Lanfranchi built the Palazzo di Città (Town Hall), the basilica of SS. Maurizio and Lazzaro, and St. Rocco; Carlo di Castellamonte planned the supremely elegant Piazza Reale, closed at one end by the churches of San Carlo and Santa Cristina; in 1658 his son Amedeo completed the façade of the Royal Palace, and in 1680 erected the tawny mass of the Ospedale Maggiore, raised the Military Academy on its solid columns and started on the Arsenal. Even before the Academy was finished an engraving by Antonio de Pienne (1675) gave a view of it, with Victor Amadeus II, then little more than a boy, in the foreground bestriding a rearing horse and looking into the distance with a fateful smile. By now Turin's inhabitants were almost 40,000; it was an active centre of trade and nobles were flocking in from the provinces attracted by the posts and amusements to be found at court. It could now be really called a town, even if in 1670 Francesco Michiel could still write that it « had nothing remarkable in it » except for Madama Reale's magnificent buildings.

The population, too, was growing with rapid and even startling bounds. The town attracted people from every part of the Savoy domains, from Savoy itself and from Nice, but especially from Piedmont, strengthening their original deep affinities and melting as it were in a crucible their characteristic vices and virtues, which throughout the centuries heredity, climate and the very soil itself had formed drop by drop like stalagmites in a cave. Thus men from every part of the country came to Turin: fair men from the Canavese, dark men from Monferrato, hard-headed inhabitants of the Langhe, sagacious peasants from Alessandria and tireless workers from Biella; vine-dressers, rice-growers, hemp-workers and tillers of the soil; herdsmen, stonemasons, truffle-hunters and frog-fishers. A rough, uncultured people, but instinctively good-natured and optimistic, poor but not famished, since corn and meat were not lacking, came to populate the little capital: and there was never a shortage of full-bodied wine from countless kinds of grape and of countless flavours to increase their natural wit in a burst of mirth and jollity.

The man who towards the end of the century was to leave the clearest imprint on the town was Guarino Guarini, the theologist, philosopher and mathematician who combined the « blazing prodigies » of the new geometry with the arcane symbols of the old decaying science and rejected both tradition and nature to express the irrationality of the merging, the sinuous dynamism and the continuous separating of forms in the whirling kaleidoscope of an unlimited space. Summoned to Turin in 1666 to complete at last the long-abandoned building of S. Lorenzo, Guarini erected the small Immacolata church next to the Archbishop's palace, the Porta di Po on the ramparts, and the Chapel of the Shroud in the Cathedral.

From the geometrical virtuosity of its plan to the daring cupola on its huge interwined arches S. Lorenzo is a sheer masterpiece. The Chapel of the Shroud is another example of striking virtuosity, a dark and sumptuous shrine glistening with black marble; but both monuments find their real expression in their interior, since the curiously close modelling of their two domes hardly dents the city's skyline.

Where Guarini has left an indelible mark on the outer face of Turin is at the crossing where the sharp angles of three of his buildings face one another at the corner of Piazza Carignano. Here the undulating mass of the Palace, as red as old mahogany warped by fire, flanks the towering buttresses of S. Filippo (its dome fallen, the price of a mad daring which defied the laws of statics!) and looks obliquely at the severe, dark and rigidly monotonous bulk of the ancient College of Nobles of the Society of Jesus. Here the local brick, only relieved by sober friezes, no longer speaks its native rustic and peasant language; it does not seek to imitate the pompous scrolls of Roman travertine, but stands foursquare, the symbol of a stern yet good-natured Subalpine despotism and the perfect expression of what was, in a well-defined historical period, the town's innermost feeling.

With the new districts extending towards the Po and Porta Susina this late baroque Turin constructs the first backdrops for the outward manifestations of sovereignty, which capable artists were to engrave *ad perpetuam rei memoriam*. To this official iconography belong Giorgio Tasnière's 31 engravings, which illustrate Venaria Reale (1674) with pictures of palaces, chapels, statues and gardens, fountains and grottoes, marble arches and avenues of trees — a theatrical setting for Arcadian dallying. In this almost abstract world the sumptuously macabre *Funeral of Charles Emmanel II* (1676) is very close — and not only in time — to the fanciful opulence of *Madama Reale's Revels* (1678), which illuminates the squares with fireworks and populates the waters of the Po with allegorical ships and benign-looking monsters. Guarini's *Architectural Designs*, too — they date from 1686 — apart from their technical perfection, are an apologia for regal munificence.

Still without the title of King — that of Cyprus was too controversial and remote to add lustre to the crown — the dynasty began on its great documentary claims: Guichenon's *Histoire généalogique* (1660) was followed in 1679 by the *Istoria dell'augusta Città di Torino* of Emanuele Tesauro, which bears on its cover — the symbol of quiet strength — a taurine Eridanus (the classical Po) with rich gifts of water and fruit; and finally in 1682, after long preparation and dogged efforts, appeared the solemn panegyric in pictures of the *Theatrum Sabaudiae*. This contains 135 folio plates — 38 devoted to Turin — which sumptuously illustrate towns and monuments in the duchy, with embellishments and amplifications that represent not merely the licence of a frivolous

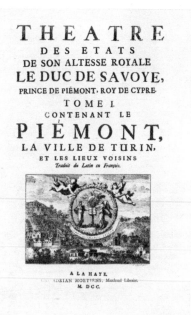

The battle of Turin of 7th September 1706 seen from the hill of Superga. Canvas attributed to Ignazio Parrocel (Turin, Muretto collection).

Medal commemorating the victory of 1706, minted at Turin: Phaeton's chariot, struck with lightning by Jupiter's eagle crashes into the Po (« Mergitur Eridano »). (Turin, Civic Museum of Ancient Art).

fancy, but the carrying out of a precise and reasoned plan (beauty and power of the domain considered as an authentic « title » to regality) and a specific promise of other works to come. So even the secret ambition finds its justifications in a moral obligation and the quest for the formal dignity prepares the way for renewal and civil progress.

Enormous and very costly to produce, the *Theatrum* was certainly distributed widely throughout the courts of Europe, and in London, Paris, Vienna and Madrid they must have thumbed it with a commiserating smile, as the bravado of a poor relation who squanders his meagre resources in trying to cut a dash. In spite of the superb bird's eye view designed by Tommaso Borgonio, Turin remained for the majority a provincial town, the capital of a precarious little Alpine state, a vassal of the omnipotent King of France. But its subjection was ended in 1703, when Victor Amadeus II severed his links with the Roi Soleil and joined the Grand Alliance. Piedmont was invaded and in spite of stubborn resistance its strong-points fell one by one, till finally in August 1705 La Feuillade's sappers began to throw a network of trenches round the last remaining bulwark of the former and now rebellious ally — Turin. In the perfect almond shape which the extensions towards the river had given it, the town dug itself in behind its sixteen bastions, its projecting ravelins and ingenious counter-defences. Defenders and powder were scarce, but not the courage determined to resist. Now indeed the town

needed all its saints: the martyrs of the Theban legion, St. Rocco, St. Francis, whom popular illustrations depicted on shining clouds in the sky of the metropolis, the tender-hearted Madonna of the Consolata, and that flesh and blood saint going round the casemates to encourage the combatants — the Blessed Sebastiano Valfré!

The eyes of all Europe were fixed on Turin. The conflict between the powers was not to be decided at Blenheim or Ramillies, Malaga or Gibraltar, but on that tongue of land between the Po and the Dora where the control of Italy, and perhaps the whole result of the long war, was at stake. On 7 September 1706 the decisive battle saw the rout of the besiegers, leaving their artillery behind them in their flight, and the rejoicing of the liberated city. The echo throughout Europe was immense. French, German and Flemish engravers produced plans and views of Turin, with the regiments deploying under fire, the smoke-laden discharge of the mortars, the mêlée of the horses, the tangle of the circumvallations and defences. A recurring feature in the copper engravings is the allegory of Phaeton: as the chariot of the Sun crashed into the Eridanus, so the star of the Roi Soleil sizzled out in the waters of the Po.

The first really radical transformation, one that was to affect not only the planning of the town but the whole composition and customs of its inhabitants, took place after the siege of 1706 and the end of the victorious war. Turin became the capital of a kingdom, healed its deep wounds and set up a meticulous and far-reaching administration. An increasingly extensive bureaucracy grew up, the nobility became urbanised, attracted by the posts and appointments to be had, while the high officials acquired titles and an aristocratic way of life. It was now that the historic centre assumed its final shape, its impress of restrained variety, sober elegance and disciplined uniformity.

Having at last obtained the royal title, Victor Amadeus II called on Filippo Juvarra to give his capital the mark of a rich but severe taste, which would express in symbols of stone all the formal pride of his new dignity. After completing the wide arcaded thoroughfare linking the Castle with the Po and laying out the long, tree-lined avenues stretching to Rivoli and Stupinigi; having erected Porta Vittoria towards the Dora and the stately and symmetrical buildings of the Porta Susina district, Juvarra rebuilt S. Filippo, decorated S. Carlo, erected S. Croce, S. Cristina and the Carmine, gave the old castle of the Acaias a regal front, built palaces for the Biragos, the Martinis and the Guarenes, and created the masterpiece of the Stupinigi hunting-lodge in the wooded plain and the basilica of Superga on the highest point of the hills. Thanks to his creative genius the whole urban nucleus received its final stamp, its definitive quality, one that unites baroque fantasy and classical composure in an austere equilibrium and military-like severity that was to be the indelible characteristic of the ancient centre of the town. When Montesquieu visited it in October 1728 he found it small — what were 50,000 inhabitants compared with the crowds of Paris? — but pleasant, well built, with straight roads, quiet gardens, noble architecture, and the various quarters « ruled with a plumb line ». And he summed up: « It is the most beautiful village in the world! ».

A few months later, contemplating the town, the plain and the majestic sweep of the mountains at dawn from the square in front of the Cappuccini church, Rousseau defined the view as « the finest picture that can strike the human eye ». Ten years after, the Président de Brosses would praise « the long straight streets, the regularity of the buildings, the beauty of the squares », but above all the absence of contrasts created elsewhere by the juxtaposition of hovels and palaces, whereas in Turin, he wrote, « there is nothing outstandingly beautiful but everything is uniform and nothing mediocre in a whole that is small but full of grace ».

Stately homes begin to rise by the dozen to house not only the owners but large indoor and outdoor staffs. Juvarra plans royal edifices, too, but the first preoccupation is to build arsenals and barracks, emphasising especially in Turin the appearance of uniformity and severe discipline that the small ambitious state is compelled to assume in order to survive, gripped as it were in a vice between Hapsburgs and Bourbons. The weight of authority became oppressive, crushing in the sphere of culture, and fundamentally levelling: no inhabitant, whether noble or commoner, could escape the royal command of « all subjects, all soldiers, all poor », which meant the suppression of the last feudal autonomies, grievous military obligations and merciless taxation for all classes.

But this did not prevent there being poor and less poor. On the contrary, the character of the town was transformed just through this more clearly defined stratification, through the fact that a parsimonious aristocracy, not unacquainted with refined pleasures and exotic fashions, lived side by side with urbanized peasants, servants, house-keepers and parasites. The opening up of spacious new suburbs, however,

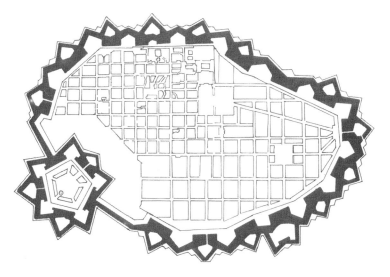

preceding plate, above:
Palazzo Carignano, one of the masterpieces of Guarino Guarini (1685). Beside it may be seen the cupola and apse of S. Filippo.

below:
A view of Piazza Castello, with the façades of the Royal Palace (the spire of the Chapel of the Holy Shroud appearing above it) and Palazzo Madama, designed by Filippo Juvarra in 1721.

Plan of Turin at the beginning of the 18th century, with the extension towards the River Po and the characteristic « almond » shape of the fortified walls.

Granatieri del Regt⁰ Guardie

Nizza Cavalleria

The splendid multi-coloured uniforms of the ancient regiments: a grenadier of the Guards and an officer of the Nizza Cavalry (Turin, Royal Library).

gave these mobs room to breathe; so the town lost its character of cheerful and noisy overcrowding and became sadder. In the large squares, in the fields outside the walls, one only saw battalions manoeuvring in close order: soldiers were everywhere, and in the streets, shops and drawing-rooms people stood with their ears strained to catch and refer to the court every rumour, every whisper in obedience to the ruthless canons of the most unenlightened reason of state. Turin gradually became more and more austere, uniform, clean and—boring.

And yet it was in this atmosphere that so much of the most genuine side of the Turinese character was indelibly shaped: a rigorous sense of discipline, a love for order carried to the point of preferring monotony to caprice, confidence in and affectionate devotion to their leaders, a feeling of duty which imposes the sacrifice of individual advantage to the common good. These are typically military virtues, which find their counterpart in a certain supine subordination, a patient endurance that seems to tend to inertia. The term « bogianén » (« one who refuses to budge ») sums up these two facets of the Subalpine temperament. Even if first uttered with a joking inflection to poke fun at a certain over-cautious and spiritless passivity, it quickly came to mean the open pride and the stubborn collective virtue of a people able to close their ranks, dig their feet in and stick in out.

To reinforce this mood Turin had a continuous influx from the valleys that debouch into its small plain of men from the mountains — chestnut-gatherers, ibex-hunters, goatherds — people accustomed to wresting a few handfuls of rye from their small stony fields and to passing interminable winters in cowsheds buried under the snow. Mountaineers, peasants, artisans thus came together to develop, in the subconscious of the popular mind, what is perhaps the most significant trait of the Piedmontese character — the ideology of work. For a large part of southern or « sunny » Italy, exhausted by the heat and drought, work has never lost its ancient Biblical connotation of primordial punishment and misfortune, when the angel with the flaming sword drove man from his earthly paradise and compelled him to earn his bread with the sweat of his brow. This does not mean, of course, that southerners are not extremely industrious people, and indefatigable workers, but that they are perpetually seeking for the unattainable bliss of a *dolce far niente* existence and are wont to identify wealth with leisure. Up here in the north, however, a keen little wind laden with Calvinist and Jansenist humours seems to blow from the mountains: here intransigence and a Puritanical strictness have nurtured the idea that toil ennobles man, that God helps them that help themselves, and that work is practical morality. Even today, after the passing of so many generations and so many events, current opinion may be indulgent towards many human weaknesses, may forgive a man for being, say, a womaniser, a gambler or a drunkard, but never a slacker or a sluggard. « A l'à nen veuja 'd travajé » (« he doesn't want to work », which is just the opposite of the triumphant, easy-going Roman « nun me va de faticà » — « work's not my line ») still remain a shameful charge, a sentence of moral ostracism.

From this dutiful and honourable sense of work there arose spontaneously a taste for careful and precise execution, an insistence on scrupulousness and excellence, an eager curiosity about technological progress, an inventive and experimental initiative. Hence, on one side, a serious, positive trait, a rejection of ostentation and muddle, a scrupulous probity, an amour-propre that is stronger than self-interest and egoism; on the other, a spontaneous understanding of the new mechanical contrivances, a practised manual ability, a disciplined patience, which were the determining prerequisites for the start of the future industrial revolution.

The Turinese vocation for the exact sciences, which drew its impulse from the military academies and the first nucleus (1757) of the Academy of Sciences seems to come from this same source and has made impressive contributions to the progress of knowledge and technological research. It is sufficient to remember the geodetic measurements and experiments with artificial electricity (1760-1774) of G. B. Beccaria, the calculus of variations (1762) and the theory of analytic functions (1797) of G. L. Lagrange, the fundamental physico-chemical law enunciated by A. Avogadro (1811), the monumental theory of the movement of the moon elaborated (1832) by G. A. Plana, G. Cavalli's invention of the rifled breech-loading gun (1844) and A. Sobrero's invention of nitro-glycerine (1847).

Populated by nobles and high officials, in the 18th century the town lost its rough edges, improved its appearance and began to acquire a refined tone. On coming into contact with an aristocracy that was neither very wealthy nor over-bearing and that spoke the same dialect, the bourgeoisie was encouraged to imitate its manners and customs, and in becoming more refined developed a certain air of spontaneous charm and smiling reserve. This was later to be known as Turinese « politeness », a blend of formal behaviour and popular common sense, of dignity and naturalness, of good manners and strict morals, which only the anonymous tide of mass incivility is now finally submerging. But the sedate and dignified « madamin », the hoydenish « totine », the young *midinettes* who were able with a mere trifle to emulate the elegance of the great ladies, remain in the memory as images of a pure, transparent world, one that was profoundly human and civilised. One at least of these figures — the « madama Basile » of the draper's in the Via Nuova — lives on immortally, beyond the reach of time which overwhelms and erases everything, in the *Confessions* of Jean-Jacques Rousseau.

Meanwhile, in the town, the works which testify to its religious piety and courtly pomp are gradually supplemented by those which reflect the cultural interests, the administrative and social affairs and the rigid centralisation of a bureaucratic and military state. The University (1720), the Public Library (1722), the Lunatic Asylum (1727), the State Archives (1734), are followed by the Secretariats and finally the Royal Theatre (inaugurated in 1740 with Metastasio's *Arsace*), which gave Piazza Castello its definitive form. Diderot and his friends would find the edifice's structure so perfect that they faithfully reproduced Benedetto Alfieri's illustrative plates (1761) in the great iconographic documentation of the *Encyclopédie*. In 1743 Marco Foscarini, the future Doge, admired

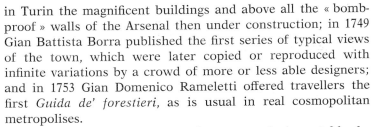

MADAMIN
de Turin en philosophe

in Turin the magnificent buildings and above all the « bomb-proof » walls of the Arsenal then under construction; in 1749 Gian Battista Borra published the first series of typical views of the town, which were later copied or reproduced with infinite variations by a crowd of more or less able designers; and in 1753 Gian Domenico Rameletti offered travellers the first *Guida de' forestieri*, as is usual in real cosmopolitan metropolises.

This « freezing » of views and prospects in immutable designs shows that the town now had a character of its own, a finished air, but it also reveals that the urge for building, the incentive for renewal, had by now slackened; in the same way that, after two centuries of alternating conflict, the expansive capacity of the old Subalpine duchy had come to a halt, as it were, on the bed of the Ticino. For the whole of the second half of the eighteenth century a regime deaf to illuministic reforms — Giannone died in 1748, victim of an ill-judged reason of state, in the Cittadella prison — seemed to perpetuate a stasis which was in reality a profound decline.

Only the military arts — mathematics, chemistry, ballistics — flourished, but on the whole there was more or less complete stagnation: culture remained poor, intellectual life was stifled, the isolation from Europe jealous and oppressive; and the innovators and rebels were either obliged to emigrate — like Alberto Radicati — or die in prison — like Dalmazzo Francesco Vasco — or else champ at the bit and curse, like the ebullient Alfieri, who felt he « breathed deeper » as soon as he managed to throw off his « native yoke » from his neck. And yet even in these men, so unusual in their vigilant insufferance and their open-mindedness towards Europe and the future, the Subalpine people's character showed its unyielding obstinacy, a determination to go their own way and a consistency even at the cost of painful sacrifices.

In the views of the time regiments parade through the squares, little men in uniform strut with a military swagger, but the spirit is no longer the same. The pictures which recur most frequently are again those once dear to the « Royal

Ladies »: theatrical performances and festivities, receptions and hunting-parties, weddings and funerals. Ignazio Sclopis del Borgo's great view (1777) shows the lifeless bastions, the squalid suburbs and, in the hills, carefree parties of ladies under pretty sun-shades. Antonio Maria Stagnon artlessly portrays the costumes of dignified « madamin » and local country-girls; Giuseppe Pietro Bagetti sketches in elegant ovals churches, bridges and castles overlooking placid waters. In a late return to Arcadia the autumn sweetness of a final idyll breathes from the hills gay with vineyards, gardens and rustic dwellings: in the *Guida alle cascine e vigne* (1791) Grossi records with the detail worthy of a land-surveyor the boundaries of five hundred villas spread over thirty miles, from Stupinigi to Leinì, from Collegno to the Eremo. Turin now had 94,000 inhabitants, innumerable hordes of beggars and much poverty: those who could sipped their wine under cool arbours, trying not to think of the future.

Then suddenly the idyll was over. In April 1796 the fragile line of the Apennines and the Bormida snapped at a blow from Bonaparte's battering ram. The harsh armistice was to be of short duration: on 7 December 1798 the French entered Turin and a troop of generals caracoled in Piazza delle Erbe flaunting their tricolor plumes. Two days later Charles Emmanuel IV sadly left the town, while a Jacobin (or perhaps merely opportunist) engraver got ready to print a view of it dated « the seventh year of the French Republic and the first of Piedmontese Liberty ». But even this liberty did not last long. The next year an Austro-Russian army besieged Turin and bombarded it with more than a hundred cannons and mortars. Stagnon no longer portrays feminine charms, but the Citadel answering the enemy fire, ablaze in the night. On 26 May 1799 Suvarov's Russians occupied Turin in an ephemeral reconquest, but no later than the following year the rout of Marengo swept them from the Po plain and on 22 June 1800 Bonaparte made his victorious entry into the capital to restore a domination that was to last for thirteen years. And indeed it was an occupation rather than a liberation. The old absolutism was overthrown, fervent Jacobins sprang up amog us too, but the new leaders never lost a certain mistrustful detachment from Paris, just as the new *citoyens* preserved a certain reluctance and irony. Many young men left to fight under the standards of the Emperor and the returning veterans later told their grandsons stories of rides and adventures across numberless frontiers, of shootings and parades, scuffles and bivouacs, moved to tears perhaps at the memory of the *petit caporal*, but continuing to regret their little fatherland and its lost freedom. We too were to see the picture of a grateful Italy kneeling at the foot of a liberating France with its caption *Matri magnae filia grata* interpreted with realistic sarcasm as « The mother eats while the daughter scrapes ».

During the Napoleonic regime the tottering civic Tower surmounted by a bronze bull bellowing to the wind fell under

the French picks, as did the glorious ramparts, transformed into tree-lined walks for the ladies and gallant officers. For the anniversary of Marengo, for the celebration of the Emperor's coronation, the architect Ferdinando Bonsignore erected the prescribed triumphal arches in correct neo-classical style, but was astute enough to make them only of wood and painted canvas and was ready three lustres later to produce the plans for the expiatory temple to the Great Mother of God offered by the governing body — now repenting of their democratic lapse — to the returning King.

On 20 May 1814, in the wake of Bubna's Uhlans, Victor Emmanuel I came to retake possession of his continental domains. He arrived from Moncalieri along the right bank of the Po, passed under a triumphal arch and rode across the imposing stone bridge which the defeated Emperor had decreed for Turin in December 1807, bringing back with him the old system and the tenets of the Holy Alliance. The Napoleonic eagle disappears from the plans and views; but the town, though impoverished and humiliated by the foreign domination, reduced to an outlying suburb, and having lost 30,000 inhabitants, seemed to recover impetus from its reacquired rank as the capital of a sovereign state which the Congress of Vienna, as a reward for its ill-fated loyalty (and out of hatred for a Jacobin republic) enriched with the sumptuous gift of the territory of Genoa.

Life was not easy or happy in the years of the Restoration, what with the reprisals of the *ci-devants*, the unbending absolutism and the compulsory devotion, in the cultural desert ensured by the censorship and the police. Pellico was able, in 1832, to print *Le mie prigioni* there, but a year later Gioberti, who was too tender towards the cause of the oppressed Poles, was to suffer prison and exile. Nevertheless, under its apparent gloom the town began to live again, to bestir itself and to work. New districts were planned, beyond Porta d'Italia and Porta Nuova; as early as 1815 the future Piazza Carlo Felice was laid out, the square that was later to constitute, together with the beginning of Via Po, the Porta Susina district and Piazza Emanuele Filiberto, the fourth monumental entrance to the town. In 1823 the contract was signed for the construction of the striking stone arch of the Mosca bridge; in 1824 the Viale del Re (Corso Vittorio Emanuele), the great ring-road to the south, was extended as far as the Po, while not far away the vast Piazza Vittorio was also extended to the river, which was thus finally brought within the city's limits. In 1827 Piazza Lagrange was opened; in 1828 Gaetano Lombardi laid out the General Cemetery; in 1831 Ignazio Michela completed the Law Courts, while in 1834 the façade of S. Carlo was faced and the Borgo Nuovo (Via Mazzini) was laid out. This was intended to fill the gap between the Viale del Re and the old fortifications.

But work also went on to complete the buildings of the Academy and the University, at the College of the Provinces and the Artillery Barracks, and every building seems to come

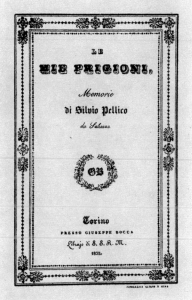

Vincenzo Gioberti. Statue in Piazza Carignano, sculptured by Giovanni Albertoni (1859).

The original edition of Pellico's « Le mie prigioni » printed at Turin in 1832.

preceding page:

The ancient Civic Tower, erected in 1382 and pulled down in 1801: plastic reconstruction (Turin, Pietro Micca Museum) and engraving by B. A. Re (1753).

Romantic views of the town.

The Mount of the Capuchins in a lithograph by Felice Festa (1817), perhaps the first print executed in Turin by this new method.

The campanile of the Cathedral in a lithograph by Villeneuve (1829). Rustic houses and artisans' shops still border on the square.

plate opposite:

A quiet corner of the old town: the garden in front of the nineteenth century wing of the Royal Palace, with ruins of Roman buildings and a surviving stretch of the walls with alternating bands of cobbles and brick. Beyond the railings, the Palatine Towers and the most important remains of the boundary wall, against a background of unpretentious 17th century houses with their characteristic dormers and long outside galleries of Luserna stone.

out of the same mould — as severe and grey as the spiritual climate in which it was born, reflecting only the administrative or social functionality that governed it, and reproducing without conviction neo-classical models in a lifeless, unadorned style which smacks of academic exercise and cautious parsimony. The general effect is of a depressing, almost prison-like barrenness. The most faithful interpreter of this unobtrusive mediocrity, which appears shabby even when on a large scale, is Giuseppe Talucchi: between 1820 and 1840 he imposed his classical temple pediments on the church of S. Filippo and the refectory of the Rosine, erected the heavy, lugubrious vault of the S. Luigi Hospital and put massive, gloomy arches between the prison-courtyards of the Lunatic Asylum. Here the austere correctness of state architecture thus reached its ultimate expression by identifying itself with funerary decoration. In the Gran Madre Bonsignore had, alas, copied the Pantheon in Rome almost stone by stone with a desolating lack of imagination, but by the grace of God approval was not given to a project of Antonelli's to raze Palazzo Madama to the ground in order to erect one of his horrible neo-classical pastiches in place of the Acaia towers and Juvarra's façade.

The iconography of this expanding town — its population was now more than 130,000 — finds an easy means of popular diffusion in Senefelder's lithographic process: as early as 1817 Felice Festa had printed from stone a view of the Monte Capuccini roughly sketched by a still inexpert hand; but Vil-

leneuve's six plates (1829) reach an almost complete mastery of the art and represent typical aspects of the city in a glare of baleful light under splendid storm-laden skies.

With Charles Albert's accession to the throne intellectual life, too, began to revive. In 1831 the Royal Library was founded, in 1834 the Armoury and Picture Gallery, and in 1840, when the second Congress of Italian scientists met in Turin, the Philharmonic Odeon and Theatrical Academy were inaugurated. The congress members were able to admire the bridge spanning the Po and, in Piazza San Carlo, the equestrian monument to Emmanuel Philibert, sculpted by Marocchetti with a skill worthy of the ancients, sparkling in its newly cast bronze. While the *homines novi* of the professions, industries, journalism and politics flocked to the capital, the burning questions of the century — the social problem and the national problem — pressed more and more urgently on the popular conscience. The long-standing sufferings of the poor and needy found common apologists and benefactors in the philanthropists and saints: Carlo Boncompagni started the kindergartens, Lorenzo Valerio denounced the harsh conditions of the workers, the « do-gooders » among the old aristocracy founded the Poorhouse and the Buon Pastore Institute, while the humble rural clergy of Piedmont, brought up to an almost Jansenist austerity, produced its hard-working saints such as Don Cafasso, who assisted prisoners, Don Cottolengo, who took in those suffering from all kinds of nameless diseases, and Don Bosco, who educated the street-urchins in the Oratory among the fields of Valdocco. Everywhere plans went ahead in a furious search for progress. In 1851 the gasometer flooded the night sky of the city with unprecedented brightness, in 1852 the « landing-stage » of the railway was opened at Porta Nuova, in 1853 the Turin-Genoa line was inaugurated and the smoke-crested locomotive crossed the Po over the new bridge at Moncalieri.

From 1848 onwards Turin was the heart of Italy, the goal of exiles awaiting the revolt; and the history of the town became identified with the history and travail of the whole country. No more palaces were built, but the first workshops for the railway lines and cannons; thus the impulse to expand was arrested once again, because other tasks became more urgent: between Via Andrea Doria and the Cavour Gardens the rectangular pattern of the streets was to remain for ever slashed across by a slanting cut, and irregular grassy mounds — stronger than the rational wills of the planners — mark the last traces of the ancient 17th century ramparts, as if the exhausted city had not completely succeeded in conquering the bank of its placid river. Although it had become a capital again after Waterloo, Turin remained more than ever a middleclass town, with the classes now in ascendancy through the manual jobs and skills being joined by a new intellectual middle class of lawyers, notaries, professors and doctors brought up to democratic ideals, interested in the experiments across the Alps, and determined to revive the old techniques and structures that had foundered at the Restoration.

Potentially, this is already the Turin of the Risorgimento, the moral capital of a divided Italy, to which exiles flocked from all parts of the country. Men of action and men of culture, they brought new life to the Subalpine city and through them the University, the publishing trade, the theatre and newspapers revived, the political question was reopened and ideas and plans of action worked out in a surge of energy in which one felt the heart of the whole nation beating. At Custoza, Novara and the Cernaia the small country paid the price of its ambitions, its immaturity and its rash obstinacy, but it held firm. And Turin was its impassioned leader, its vital nerve centre. Even if, in the light of rigorous and unbiased historical research the popular myths which served to induce a divided and unprepared Italy to accept the unitary Savoy monarchy are exploded, here in the north the undoubted fact remains of a genuine participation by the people, of a deep understanding — in spite of so many reasons for dissension — between the cultured, radical and democratic middle class and the old forces of the enlightened aristocracy, the bureaucracy and the army. A large number of the common people came out into the streets in the winter of 1847, with cudgels under their cloaks, to demand the Constitution and, two years later, their guns in their hands, to agitate for a war to the death. And it was common people that formed the old brigades of infantry, the field batteries, the cavalry squadrons which, after long periods of service, bloody battles and harsh discipline returned to their homes with a new self-respct and a modest pride, whether they felt it was a duty done or through conviction (even if imaginary) of their superiority over the defeated Austrian or Papal troops. In their long service and hard-won experience as soldiers they discovered a human dignity and manly pride they had not known before, and this, mingling with their native love for liberty, opened their eyes to the most serious problem of the new times — the political and social question.

In the Piedmontese character this sense of military glory has remained like a vein of secret pride and convinced superiority, not paraded only because it is considered indisputable. No one today probably remembers Assietta, San Martino or Porta Pia, but it only needs a squad of Alpini to march past with their plumes waving or a fanfare of Bersaglieri bugles to ring out for hearts to beat a little faster. And it is not military arrogance or bellicose nostalgia but the sense of a tradition of fidelity and efficiency, the pride in a legendary pre-eminence, the awareness of belonging to some peaceful, taciturn, unemotional people, suspicious of all rhetoric and even slow-witted, but able to work and suffer, shoulder to shoulder, faithful to the simple traditional values of their fathers.

The squalid « House of the Red Vault » in Via Palazzo di Città, where in 1828 St. Giuseppe Cottolengo founded his « Little House of the Divine Providence » with four beds.

The monument to St. John Bosco by Gaetano Cellini (1920), erected in front of the Salesian basilica of Maria Ausiliatrice.

Piedmontese infantry leaving for the front march past the church of S. Filippo and the Science Academy. Tempera by Carlo Bossoli (1859). The severe baroque and neo-classical architecture, the sun shining through the clouds, the disciplined ranks of the troops and the unrestrained enthusiasm of the crowds admirably convey the tension of a historic moment and the city's deepest feelings.

opposite page:

Turin's final sacrifice for the unification of Italy was the painful renunciation of the rank of capital: popular indignation was repressed by force of arms.

The sanguinary riot in Piazza San Carlo on the evening of 22nd September 1864. Sketch by Ettore Giacomelli published in « L'Illustration » of Paris.

At the 1865 Carnival the masker Gianduia expresses the city's devotion to its King in Piazza San Carlo. Lithograph by Felice Cerruti.

After the early enthusiasms, the sacrifices and defeats of 1848 and 1849 the busy decade of preparation suddenly matured in the spring of 1859. The brigades of infantry in their blue jackets, the cavalry regiments with their glorious names, paraded through the ancient streets to a great tinkling of swords and lances. In anxious trepidation the population saluted the King as he calmly left for the battlefield. It then waited for news of losses and victories, rejoiced at S. Martino, cursed Villafranca, and gave a delirious welcome to the exultant survivors. Then events moved towards solutions beyond every expectation and hope: the Kingdom of Sardinia became the Kingdom of Italy, but Turin was too out of the way, too exposed, too near to France for it to be the capital of a united nation for whom Rome was an inspiring symbol. In 1864, when the September Convention decreed the transfer of the capital to Florence, Turin, wounded to the heart, felt herself flouted and betrayed and rose in a fury

of exasperation. But the crowd that came out to riot in Piazza S. Carlo was cut down by musket fire: 187 citizens fell under this act of repression and the city resigned itself, albeit with profound bitterness, to the unjust abdication and the dreary future awaiting it — that of vegetating as the capital of an outlying province, deprived of all power and dignity, in an obscure mediocrity.

But the humiliation and grief had to be swallowed; new ways had to be found. To the minister Menabrea, who had proposed in the name of the Minghetti government that an indemnity should be paid to Turin, the mayor Rorà replied with scornful pride: « Turin is not for sale. If the transfer is necessary for the good of the country, why speak of compensation? » At the carnival of the following year, one of

the Gianduia maskers in his shirt sleeves went up to the King, who was passing through the square in his carriage, and symbolically offered him his shirt with the words: « For Italy and for you ».

Once the thrilling episode of independence and unity was past, the legend of valour and dedication to the country had paled and the last sacrifice had been made, it was as though the lights on the stage had gone out. The court departed and with it the Parliament, the embassies, the ministries and the high command; abruptly the population fell by 30,000: the whole life of the city seemed to stop.

The small and compact historic nucleus of the bureaucratic and military capital of the Savoy state had outlived its function; the ruthless logic of national unity deprived Turin of its pre-eminent position to relegate it to that isolated cul-de-sac of the western Alps which, after having been its defence for centuries, now seemed as if they must become its prison. Not only did Turin pay to the last farthing the high price of the country's redemption, but very soon it saw the very spirit of its labour and sacrifice rejected, because a united Italy took over its external, dynastic and military affairs, but spurned its profoundly educative and disciplinary vocation, its Jansenistic seriousness and its call to make, not only Italy, but the Italians.

It was above all this fundamental rejection (the tragic symbol, ultimately, of a Giolitti defeated by a Salandra) that was to attribute to the men who had grown up in a climate such as ours the charge of offensive rudeness, lack of communicativeness and tiresome meddling. In the new capital their stiff, monotonous buildings round an ugly, arcaded square introduced a foreign, uncouth note, as depressing through its lack of invention as its Subalpine nostalgia was pathetic. Seen from the viewpoint of Rome, Turin rapidly sank to a provincial level, not only because it was outlying and remote, but because it was hard to assimilate and « different ».

As thousands of bureaucrats and soldiers left it and so many activities ceased, the town appeared as if stunted. Isolated, humiliated, stung to the quick, Turin seemed to be on the way to a dignified, if calm, decline; it was almost as if it wished to become like an impoverished *grande dame*: it decked itself with shady avenues, it opened smart shops, it welcomed important retired officials and generals in a polite, aristocratic atmosphere. For in the first decades after the unification of Italy the senior representatives of the civil service, often Piedmontese by birth or education, the old generals who had been trained in their youth in the classrooms of the Academy in Via della Zecca, almost all returned to Turin to enjoy their meagre pensions quietly in the new residential districts of the Borgo Nuovo stretching to the Po, or of the old Piazza d'Armi and the Crocetta, in the dignified but unpretentious new houses, spending their time at the old cafés or walking along the avenues in the shade of the horse-

chestnuts. It was they who gave the Turin of the turn of the century — the Turin of De Amicis, Giacosa, the Calandra brothers — its formal and reserved atmosphere, made up of right feelings and good manners, of faith in institutions and the cult of the past.

So, in a climate of respectability and decorum filled with glorious memories and nostalgia for its vanished little fatherland, a whole world moved slowly towards an inexorable decline. But Turin did not die with it, in fact from year to year it seemed to discover new energies and, as it were, its more genuine face. With the dynastic pomp forgotten, the military trophies put away, the political question settled, the city that had been so abruptly despoiled and humiliated seemed to reveal its hidden strength. In the shabby suburbs, in the dark, gloomy houses of the centre, a humble and patient people now clustered together, numerous, compact and united. Shepherds from the barren mountain valleys, vinedressers from the impoverished Langhe, transplanters of rice from the plain, bricklayers and tinsmiths from the foothills of the Alps, all came to the city in search of bread. A rough, quiet people, one accustomed to hard labour and with a love for careful, serious, faultless workmanship. They were peasants who had become smiths and weavers, coach-builders and leather-workers, joiners and printers; and by 1865 there were tens of thousands of them. On the threshold of the industrial era Turin housed this enormous potential reserve of honest craftsmanship, this availability of labour, this capacity for exemplary work. The sense of responsibility and managerial ability were not lacking either, and the whole city turned to industry and work in search of salvation — and perhaps unconscious revenge. Twenty years later, the 1884 Exhibition already showed signs of the recovery, the will to survive by a city which refused to be relegated to the margins of the country and claimed its function as a leader in a new field.

Dreariness of the industrial suburbs and the squalid tenements of the 19th century. The red chimneys and the metal frames of the gasometers stand out against the smoky sky; the blocks of workers' houses press round the factories: rows of isolated rooms, without sanitation, overlook dismal courtyards.

The monument to Galileo Ferraris by Luigi Contratti (1902) in the avenue bearing his name.

The issue for 22nd April 1888 of « L'Elettricità » in which Galileo Ferraris announced his discovery of the rotating magnetic field.

Beyond the leafy belt of broad avenues created on the ruins of the ancient ramparts, the nineteenth century workers' town of the « barriere » and the « borghi » gradually grew up round the old historic centre and the quiet residential districts. It was made up of dreary sheds that soon became grimy, of smoking chimneys, and of tenement buildings where the wretched lodgings were ringed with long stone balconies. Around the aristocratic Turin of the 18th century, the frigid Turin of the Restoration, rose the poor Turin of the workers: the « Cà neire », the « Borg d'el fum », the « Barriera » of Milan, and those of Nizza, Vanchiglia and Lingotto, Lucento and Madonna di Campagna — a grey, shabby urban network which only the exemplary pattern of the ancient nucleus saved from an irreparable deterioration. In those beehive-like buildings were housed the hundred thousand poor, the seventy thousand illiterates who were there to guarantee Turin a new future through their work and suffering. The sons of mountain folk, needy peasants, servants, labourers, they had only the strength of their arms and their traditional patience; they brought to their workshops the manual experience of their simple old-fashioned trades of wheelwrights, millers, umbrella-makers, knife-grinders, farriers and spinners. In town they all became industrial workers. In the arsenal they learnt to cast guns, to laminate rails for the railways, to work steel and copper; they soon became familiar with the new processes and machines as the industrial revolution laboriously got under way. The traditional local resource of silk-manufacture still took first place — in 1866 Turin had 36 silk-mills and 2,300 looms in operation — but there were already 21 metallurgical workshops and there was a rapid increase in wool and cotton mills, and chemical industries producing waxes and soaps, oils and asphalt, and raising the towers of gasometers. Other factories tanned hides, quarried stone and dug peat, worked jute and made paper. A position of particular importance was acquired by the graphic arts, with 40 printing-works, 14 lithographic presses, 5 type-foundries: everywhere new sheds appeared and the red chimneys of boilers and furnaces struck the eye.

In 1865, the very year when the capital was moved to Florence, the Workers' General Association was started in Turin; in 1868 the members of the Mutual Aid Society were already 27,000; in 1891 the Chamber of Trade was founded. Three years before, in two modest pages of a small technical newspaper, Galileo Ferraris had announced to the world the discovery of the rotating magnetic field, the prerequisite of the electric motor and the great industrial urban concentrations of the 20th century. The little professor did not jealously protect with patents the intuition that had struck him like a flash one day when he was walking and day-dreaming near the Cernaia barracks. He, too, was of peasant stock and with idealistic fervour made his gift to humanity. But above all he made it to Turin, which, in its position at the foot of the Alpine valleys, became at one stroke mistress of the intangible power of their waters and the mysterious energy which could at last be transmitted and used at a distance.

In this way, therefore, Turin became more and more a capital of labour, a town of technicians and factory-hands, with all their struggles and hopes, coloured by humanitarian socialism. It was the mouthpiece for proletarian claims, fought hard trades union battles, underwent the harshest strikes, and slowly won more humane living conditions for its growing masses of workers. In this climate of burning disputes and laborious progress the Subalpine character did not change, in fact it seemed to recognise itself more completely in the new times that were coming and to adapt itself to them with complete naturalness. The love for serious work well done, pride in the technical difficulty overcome and the faultless product remained; as did the ancient devotion and silent discipline. But the dynastic and military aspects faded, while on the contrary the solidarity of the social group increased, together with the duty to take part in the common effort, the capacity to subordinate individual interests — or lack of them — to the demands of a majority united in its needs and hopes. The ancient *bonhomie*, made up of common sense and a kind heart, remained too, with flashes of wit and carefreeness (the picnic in the hills, the game of bowls under the pergola, the glass of wine with friends, the old songs) but the rustic simplicity was by now tempered by the townsman's shrewdness; it had lost its naïveté and become wary. The ancient dialect lost ground under the unrelenting pressure of literary Italian: its expressive vocabulary became impoverished, but retaliated by turning Italian words into dialect, recovering slang terms, words from the jargon of crafts or the underworld, with a vitality of invention that never slackened. There remained the long-suffering patience, the ability to endure, a sort of wilful obstinacy which, in an age of freer initiative and greater opportunity, set into a rock-like solidity of purpose, an aptitude to face difficulties and pay the consequences, which is the primary characteristic of numberless small and great initiators — shabby, tireless and even ruthless — and great makers and acquirers of wealth.

Once the faded trophies were laid aside Turin had recognised its true vocation and put itself in the forefront of the « industrial revolution » in Italy, despite a terrain deprived of natural resources and shut in by rigid geographical barriers, so that for decades it was faced with the prospect of intensive development only in the field of agriculture. In this way its small territory was gradually transformed into a kind of large factory in which 4% of the Italian population now produces 6% of the country's income.

Thus the old capital of the kingdom of Sardinia successively became the capital of the confectionery, motor car, cinema, telephone and radio industries, always open to new opportunities for increasing wellbeing and to future possibi-

The quiet, friendly game of bowls under the trees of surburban inns.

Views of Turin at the dawn of the 20th century:

The luxurious Ghersi Cinema in the old Via Roma, demolished after 1931 to widen the main artery.

The first Fiat factory in Corso Dante at the beginning of the 20th century.

The Umberto I Gallery near Porta Palazzo.

opposite page:
The first car built by Fiat in 1899: the « 3½ HP » model.

lities, and always humiliated by the ill-conceived imperatives of centralisation, enforced renunciations and unjust deprivations. But at the same time the city remained a capital of culture, a lively centre for experiment and discussion, a stronghold of civilised dignity and freedom. In its darkest hours were to ring out — discordant yet fraternal — the voices of Gobetti and Gramsci, Ruffini and Einaudi, inflexible witnesses of uncompromising refusal and stubborn hope.

At this point the Turin of history merges with the Turin of today, which it is no longer possible to regard with serene detachment since every picture evokes a memory, a moment of intense participation, since the thousand-year-old city becomes completely identified with the city of one's childhood — with the Belgian company's small trams rattling along in the snow, the cast-iron fountains pouring out the icy water of the Pian della Mussa reservoir from the nostrils of the copper-green bull, the sign of the cup of steaming chocolate under the Umberto I Gallery, the fluttering curtains of the cool outside cafés along the boulevards, the pink marble of the Ghersi cinema and the grey cement of the monumental stadium, the old woman selling hot chestnuts under the arcades of Via Po and the shop that sold leeches in Via S. Tommaso... But even this working-class Turin, poor to the point of dreariness but proud of its labours, now seems gone for ever. The girdle of factories and tenements was reduced to ashes in the nights of the Apocalypse, when from the ridge of Moncalieri I saw its unprotected sky illuminated by the bluish flash of the incendiaries, and then the whole plain lit up like an enormous bonfire as churches and buildings burned, ancient walls were destroyed and impotence and love filled the heart with a desperate rage.

But the recovery took place with lightning speed, the wounds have very largely healed and the city has, as it were, exploded in an unrestrainable expansion. As far as the eye can see, along the avenues laid out where up to yesterday there were meadows and fields, there now rise towering blocks of flats, factories as neat and pretty as villas, and the consumer civilisation — anonymous, proliferating, irresistible — seems to be trying to erase any distinguishing feature, to reduce all history to an ephemeral present. For more than ten years running, fifty thousand immigrants a year have come here in search of wellbeing and security, and to all of them the town has given work, and with work houses, schools, hospitals and a measure of civilisation, an example that is unobtrusive but none the less eloquent and decisive. Many of their children already speak our spirited dialect, and already think in terms of Subalpine common sense, and the old and new citizens work, study and research together in active harmony, the authentic *avant garde* of a country that from this its furthest corner breaks through the centuries-old barrier of the Alps and looks confidently to the Europe of tomorrow.

For centuries the capital of a pluri-national state held together by a common civilisation of mountain peoples, relegated to the borders of Italy, it is in this new Europe that Turin recognises itself and finds once more its ancient vocation. The new dimension brings it back to the centre of the communications and industrial system, standing four-square on the 45th parallel which, lying as it does halfway between the pole and the equator, is almost the symbol of a difficult balance between the love for work and the pleasure of living, between an intense nordic vocation and a deep responsibility towards the south that is, after all, Italy. Its provincial destiny becomes a cosmopolitan one and the Turinese's double nature adapts itself to it: homely under the arcades of its towns and villages and daring in its undertakings throughout the four continents.

Turin remains pre-eminently the « city of the motor car », the Italian Detroit; but a still lively spirit of enterprise continually tends to balance the dense industrial concentrations with a swarm of auxiliary and autonomous undertakings rich in dynamic energy, and every year the crowded exhibitions are like huge show windows full of products of high quality for an active market of international trade.

Cultural interests, too, remain strong and in the most varied fields, ranging from literature and publishing, the theatre and music, to the University and museums — the close links of a chain in which the works of philosophers, artists and men of letters meet in a common climate of high seriousness and civilised participation. They include those who have died recently but are still alive in the memory and by their example, such as Persico and Solari, Casorati and Spazzapan, Monti and Cosmo, Ginzburg and Pavese, and the many who, alive and active, daily renew a tradition of work which goes deep and who are tendentially averse to publicity and applause.

In its fortunate natural environment the city seems to be expanding today with a tumultuous and unrestrainable force. It already includes twenty-three communes in its metropolitan area and another twenty-nine are linked in a far-reaching network of communications and trade, while a system of motorways and tunnels extends towards the growing industrial conurbations of the Rhone, the Seine and the Rhine. The city, in fact, is a real megalopolis projected towards the future, teeming with problems, fraught with tensions, but confident in its traditional seriousness and proud hopes. A few years ago, in a moment of perhaps ephemeral prosperity and optimism, some Turinese went so far as to toy with the

Piles of rubble in the centre of the town as a result of the air bombardments during the Second World War.
The town has been able to heal a large part of its wounds, but the damage suffered in the insane conflict was enormous and sometimes irreparable.

opposite page:

The new expanse of modern factories which stretch as far as the eye can see round Turin, the capital of work.

apocalyptic vision of building an « Acropolis », a projected administrative centre with glass towers 120 metres high, « silos » for 30,000 motor cars, underground railways, moving carpets for pedestrians, huge hanging gardens: a science fiction future which, it seemed, could begin tomorrow.

Today a polluted ecology, the sources of power exhausted, and the embittering of international and social divisions seem to invite caution and retreat, which may even be seen as the fruits of wisdom, provided they do not in reality conceal a narrowness of view and a tendency to live from day to day. However, the city's problem, today, is not so much that of its anonymous and disfiguring growth, but the answer to a subtler question, namely, to what extent, in the future, can Turin remain itself? How long can its urban civilisation — so strongly assimilative in spite of the ebb and flow of internal migration and the levelling effect of mass communications — succeed in salvaging something of the tenacious psychological and moral character and the traditional customs of its people? Perhaps the city of history, the one which was still for me the city of my childhood, is about to end, as it must do in the levelling and anonymous age towards which we are moving — an age hypnotised by the erotic publicity and edulcorated information of the mass media, unified by the standardised models of fashion and the popular idols, so mixed by the large-scale migrations as to lose any individuality it may have had, and levelled by mass production, psychological conditioning and the unflagging growth of waves of humanity all aspiring to security and comfort, but increasingly incapable of effective self-government.

Turin suffers the acutest evils of this mass civilisation at the very moment when it is reaping its greatest material benefits. An immigration so massive that it has doubled the population in less than twenty years would have overwhelmed any other city and made it lose its identity: yet Turin has resisted the shock and up to a point remains itself. It is not just chance that among the hosts of workers who have come up from the South the most numerous are the Apulians, the most silent and disciplined of our Southern lands, the tenacious « ant-like people » who suffer least from the sudden change from an archaic rural economy to the automation of the great industrial metropolises. It is not just chance that in no other city has the assimilation of the new settlers been so rapid, spontaneous and total, as if the model for a new society with different customs succeeds better in this climate of unassertive reserve, which does not impose a new discipline but suggests a more complex civilisation. The near future — town-planners and statisticians tell us — will see a single industrial conurbation stretching from Turin to Venice, a frightening tangle of cement and glass, completely depersonalised and uniform; and this in its turn will be identical with other megalopolises in every part of the world, those in which technocrats will oblige us to live meditating a planned and sterilised happiness like automata. The Turin of yesterday, even the Turin of today, both old and new, that still survives, will be no more than a memory. But if mankind is to salvage something at least of the tormented and glorious *humanitas* of its past, it will be able to do so only thanks to the simple and courageous virtues — patience, good will, respect, trust, cheerfulness — which here for centuries have marked the peoples of the « flat country at the foot of the mountains » and been the most genuine spirit of the humble and disciplined town which they created on the bank of the placid river, between the green of the hills and the majestic amphitheatre of the Alps.

A Turin still fresh and green, not swallowed up by cement.
The loop of the Po above the town, between the Valentino Park (left) and the last offshoots of the hills. Ancient trees and new factories are mirrored in the placid river.
In the foreground the Franco Balbis bridge (1928) followed by the Princess Isabella bridge (1881) and the monumental Umberto I bridge (1907).

following pages:

A sweeping aerial view of the city from the east against the majestic, protective background of the Alps crowned by perpetual snow. In the foreground Borgo Po, on the right bank of the river, clustering round the neoclassical church of the Great Mother of God, completed in 1831. Beyond it, the Napoleonic bridge (1810-1814), dedicated to Victor Emmanuel I, the vast Piazza Vittorio

Veneto (1830) and Via Po, completed at the beginning of the 18th century. To the left Borgo Nuovo, which grew up round the middle of the 19th century with Corso Cairoli fronting the river. To the right, the broad artery of Corso S. Maurizio, built on the line of the ancient bastions, separates the Royal Gardens (over which towers the Mole Antonelliana, 1863-1897) from the Vanchiglia district, which stretches as far as the mouth of the Dora.

left, above:

The leafy Royal Gardens, the Mole Antonelliana, its incredibly slender spire visible in all the views of the city, and the northern suburbs beyond the Dora.

below:

Piazza Statuto (1864) at the exit from the old town on the road to France, with the end of Via Garibaldi and the monument commemorating the piercing of the Mont Cenis tunnel (1879).

above:

The Cathedral of St. John Baptist (1496) with its unprepossessing little dome and sturdy bell-tower (1470) capped by the belfry added by Filippo Juvarra in 1722. Behind the Cathedral, the Royal Palace (1658), the work of Amedeo di Castellamonte, with the vaguely eastern cupola of the Chapel of the Holy Shroud designed by Guarino Guarini in 1682 backing onto the sacred edifice. The remains of the ancient Roman theatre are clearly visible near the bell-tower.

above:

The Valentino Castle (1630-1660), with its pointed roofs in the French style, in the heart of the park of the same name, between the broad highway of Corso Massimo d'Azeglio and the quiet waters of the Po.

right:

Piazza Carlo Felice (1847), severely neo-classical, with its garden of rare trees, and the line of the new Via Roma, rebuilt between 1931 and 1937 wider than the 17th century Via Nuova and with the addition of arcades.

View of the city from the nearby
Observatory of the Monte dei
Cappuccini. The tall, cold neo-classical
buildings of Piazza Vittorio Veneto
and the Napoleonic bridge over the
Po are clearly seen, with the Mole
Antonelliana standing out against the
impressive background of the blue
and white chain of the Alps.

Turin

pictures of yesterday and today

The bare and severe sixteen-sided towers, thirty metres high, of the Palatine Gate (1st century A. D.) — the ancient « Porta principalis dextera » — the most remarkable edifice surviving from Roman Turin and the most ancient and important among the monuments of this type which have come down to us in the whole Empire. Two wider arches in the two-storeyed wall between the towers were for vehicles and two smaller ones for pedestrians. The bronze statues are recent copies.

Roman brick foundations of the ancient Decuman Gate in the vaults and inside the medieval facing of the two western towers of Palazzo Madama, today hidden by the splendid 18th century façade.

51

Remains of the Roman theatre and base of a tower at the side of the sanctuary of **Maria Consolatrice**. Built in the 1st century A. D. and later enlarged, the Theatre preserves its semicircular auditorium, artificially raised and levelled, and remains of the « orchestra » and the « pulpitum ».

The solid Romanesque campanile of the church of Sant'Andrea (11th century), today incorporated in the sanctuary of Maria Consolatrice, known through the people's devotion to it as « La Consolata ».

Pathetic figures of other times in a corner of the old town: the umbrella-mender.

The austere façade in terracotta of the
church of S. Domenico, begun in 1227.
In the interior, of early Gothic
construction, are preserved fragments
of 14th century frescoes and the
« Madonna of the Rosary »
by Guercino.

opposite page, above:
The large groundfloor hall in the
eastern extension of Palazzo Madama
built by Ludovico d'Acaia in the second
decade of the 15th century.

below:
The medieval towers of Palazzo
Madama, with its curious trapezoidal
plan, the lower foundations of which
are formed by the ancient Decuman
Gate. On the left may be seen one of
the squat Roman towers incorporated
in the 18th century reconstruction.

Rare surviving example of 15th-16th
century civil architecture in
Via IV Marzo, with the flat-topped,
cross-barred windows in terracotta and
the depressed arches over the entrance
to the shops.

Fishermen on the Po: another picture
of old times, when the industrial
civilisation had not yet polluted the
water and killed all life in the river.
In the 16th century sturgeon
weighing five kilos could still be
caught in it.

plate opposite:

An apparition from the waters of the
river, as unreal as a mirage.
The Medieval Village in the Valentino,
a historical reconstruction directed
by Alfredo d'Andrade for the National
Exhibition of 1884.
A neo-Gothic taste, a love for
historical memories and the
craftsman's insistence on perfect
execution meet in this faithful
and evocative « copy » inspired by
authentic models, especially
of the Valdostan castles of Issogne
and Fénis.

opposite page:
The Cathedral, dedicated to St. John
the Baptist, was erected between 1491
and 1496 to the orders of Cardinal
Domenico della Rovere, Archbishop
of Turin, on the site of three
demolished churches of the 6th-7th
centuries (St. Salvator, St. John and
St. Mary « de Dompno »). Designed
by a humble Tuscan architect, Meo
del Caprina of Settignano, the
building clearly reveals Albertian
influences, but above all copies in dull
and slavish form the Florentine façade
of S. Maria Novella. On the other
hand the marble carvings which adorn
the pilaster strips and jambs of the
portals are extremely fine.

The elegant courtyard of Palazzo
Scaglia di Verrua (Via Stampatori 4)
preserves traces of ancient frescoes.
In spite of some unfortunate
alterations it remains the only example
in Turin of civil architecture of the
late 16th century.

The small church with a central plan
of St. Mary on the Monte dei
Cappuccini, a low hill on the right
bank of the Po, where a redoubt
was built to defend the only bridge.
The church was erected between
1585 and 1596, on models favoured by
Tuscan Mannerism, by Ascanio
Vittozzi of Orvieto, who was active
in Turin for some thirty years and
died there in 1615. Vittozzi was
responsible for the first systematic
planning of the town with the
construction of regular arcaded
buildings round Piazza Castello and
the opening up of the first stretch
of Via Nuova (Via Roma).

Figures from a simple, peaceful past:
the itinerant photographer in the
Valentino, at the foot of the
monument to Massimo d'Azeglio.

opposite page:

The church and monastery of the
Monte dei Cappuccini. From the
arches of the loggia the view ranges
over the city and the distant
mountains.

Stalls of secondhand books under the trees of Corso Siccardi. The avenue, called after the minister who was responsible for the law abolishing the ecclesiastical courts in 1850, covers the area of the ancient Citadel.

As soon as he had won back his dominions and established his capital at Turin, Emmanuel Philibert decided to erect an impregnable fortress there. It was planned by Francesco Paciotto, a native of Urbino, with the collaboration of Francesco Orologi of Vicenza, in the form of a large pentagon defended by a complex system of bastions, moats and entrenchments which made it one of the best fortified strongholds in Europe. The site chosen was the south-west corner of the old Roman and medieval curtain-wall, since it was the least protected by natural defences. The first stone was laid on 2nd September 1564 and four years later the work was completed in its essential structures. Unfortunately the huge construction (a faithful plastic reproduction of which is shown on the opposite page) was demolished as the result of the development plans of 1857. Only the last redoubt, the « Mastio » (above), now enclosed in a small garden, was spared. Since 1893 it has housed the National Artillery Museum, founded in 1731 and rich in firearms of every period, uniforms, standards and trophies.

The façade and courtyard of the Valentino Castle, erected between 1630 and 1660 by Carlo di Castellamonte and his son Amedeo, on the site of a less imposing ducal residence already existing there in the middle of the 16th century. The edifice remained outside the perimeter of the town until the second half of the 19th century and is today surrounded by the Park which bears its name, a favourite playground for children.

plate opposite:

The east front in bare brick of the Valentino Castle, on the banks of the Po. It now houses the Faculty of Architecture, but when Madama Reale brought it to its present form, in the middle of the 17th century, the splendid building was intended to provide a refined setting for courtly entertainments.

A rustic landing-stage on the leafy banks of the Po. Oarsmen still hold their races on its quiet waters, almost undisturbed by the spread of the new mass amusements, noisier but less energetic.

The « Queen's Villa », on a slope of the hills overlooking the city. Cardinal Maurizio of Savoy, the youngest child of Charles Emmanuel I, purchased the land in 1617 to build himself a retreat where he could pursue his literary studies. Vittozzi may have made the first plans for it, but the present building was largely created about the middle of the 17th century under the direction of Amedeo di Castellamonte; it was reconstructed a century later by Ignazio Agliaudi di Tavigliano, a continuator of Juvarra. Frescoes and decorations by notable masters are preserved in the interior. The name comes from the fact that the building was the favourite residence of the first Savoy Queen: Anne of Orleans, the wife of Victor Amadeus II.

Since 1869 the Villa has housed the Institute for Officers' Daughters; theatrical performances are held in its park, like the one by the Young People's Experimental Theatre shown here.

opposite page:
The theatrically ornate belvedere in the park of the Queen's Villa.

Another pleasant aristocratic residence on the outskirts of the town: the Villa della Tesoreria in Corso Francia, built in 1714 for the King's Treasurer General, Aimo Ferrero di Cocconato, to the designs of the Theatine monk, Iacopo Maggi. The edifice, now municipal property, has a large central saloon and various frescoed rooms; in the park, rich in exotic trees, children play.

Piazza San Carlo, worthy of its ancient name of Piazza Reale, was created in 1640 in the centre of the first extension of the town's limits along the axis of the Via Nuova, to the plans of Carlo di Castellamonte. The perfect harmony of the whole is still further accentuated by the contrasts of light and shade in the façades of the twin churches which, like ornate baroque wings of a stage, close the vast rectangular space to the south. On the left, S. Cristina, erected in 1639, has a façade of sculpturesque relief designed by Filippo Juvarra in 1715. On the right S. Carlo's is a dignified copy of it (1834) by Ferdinando Caronesi, though in fact the church had been the first to rise in the new quarter in 1619.

below:

The second order and pediment of Juvarra's façade.

Two monolithic edifices of strict uniformity flank Piazza S. Carlo; these are divided into equal but pleasing sections, further enhanced by decorative reliefs of sober elegance.

The façades originally rested on pairs of open columns, which gave the base an appearance of lightness in more pronounced contrast with the compact mass of the two upper storeys; the effect of inversion

of the volumes was analagous to that of the Doge's Palace at Venice. But in the second half of the 18th century it was necessary to fill in the space between the columns to strengthen the pilasters.

The Royal Palace, erected on the site where ancient ducal and episcopal residences had long stood, has a façade designed in 1658 by Amedeo di Castellamonte. It faces the quiet Piazzetta Reale, which the heavy cast iron railing designed by Pelagio Palagi in 1835 separates from Piazza Castello. Equestrian statues of the Dioscuri, modelled by Abbondio Sangiorgio in 1846, face each other on the two pilasters flanking the entrance.

Piazza Palazzo di Città, the ancient Piazza delle Erbe, which had existed since the 14th century in front of the municipal buildings, began to assume its present appearance in 1756 thanks to a project by Benedetto Alfieri, which repeats Juvarra's design for the military Headquarters and in particular the nearby opening of Via Milano into the present Piazza della Repubblica.

The arcades of Piazza S. Carlo, the smart meeting place under the 17th century vaults.

The City Hall, in the heart of the oldest part of the town, was built by Francesco Lanfranchi in 1659 and enlarged several times in the following century. The bronze group by Pelagio Palagi (1853) commemorating the exploits in the East of Amadeus VI of Savoy, known as the Green Count, stands out against the façade.

The Greater Hospital of St. John
Baptist, an austere mass of dark
brick, was begun in 1680 to the
designs of Amedeo di Castellamonte,
who died the same year. It was
continued by Gianfrancesco Baroncelli
and Michelangelo Garove and was
considerably enlarged several times
up to the middle of the 18th century
and even later.

opposite page:

In 1682-3 Baroncelli also built the
beautiful palace of the Marquis
Marc'Antonio Graneri della Roccia
in Via Bogino, today the quarters of
the Artists' Club. The building is
noted for its imposing vestibule and
and the severe square staircase,
perhaps inspired by designs
by Guarini.

A decisive contribution to baroque architecture in Turin was that given by Guarino Guarini (1624-1683) of Modena, summoned by the Fathers of his order — the Theatine — to build the church of S. Lorenzo, which was constructed between 1668 and 1680. An inexhaustible inventor of spaces defined by mathematical formulae and enlivened by twists, intersections and polycentric radiations, Guarini conceived this, his first Turinese masterpiece, as a convex-sided octagon, with a double order of arches pierced by multiple window lights culminating in the fantastic star-shaped dome supported on eight slender entwined ribs, the models for which are to be sought in the great examples of medieval Arab architecture like the mosque of Cordoba. The church has no façade, as it is inserted in Vittozzi's uniform division of the buildings in Piazza Castello; only the dome rises above the roofs with its characteristic large oval windows decorated with curling scrolls like coats of arms. From the interior the fanciful eight-pointed star displays its strict geometry that dissolves in the light.

plate opposite:

The monument to Emmanuel Philibert, the work of Carlo Marochetti (1838) and a masterpiece of 19th century statuary, stands out in Piazza S. Carlo between the façades of the churches of S. Cristina and S. Carlo.

opposite page:

One of Sangiorgio's Dioscuri bestrides his rearing horse in front of the pile of Guarini's S. Lorenzo.

Palazzo Carignano, another of the Turinese masterpieces of Guarini, was started in 1679 and finished in 1685 for Emmanuel Philibert of Savoy Carignano, called the Silent. The edifice, which was completed by Baroncelli, has as its dominant theme the atrium and the saloon of the piano nobile over it, of an unusual elliptic form: this central motif determines both the sinuous movement of the façade, which matches it with its dynamic undulations, and the encircling curve of the two staircases.

The small church of the Immaculate Conception adjoining the Archiepiscopal palace, erected between 1673 and 1697 to a design by Guarini. The dramatic façade, like the thin, veined sheet of an unrolled drawing is typical.

opposite page:
The curving staircase of Palazzo Carignano, decorated with oval niches enclosed in scrolls, typical of Guarini's taste in ornamentation.

The Chapel of the Holy Shroud, at the centre of the wing of the Royal Palace that adjoins the Cathedral, is Guarini's most original and fascinating work as well as being one of the greatest masterpieces of European baroque. Conceived in 1668, crowned with its dome in 1682, it was completed twelve years later with the sumptuous altar by Antonio Bertola. In it is kept the linen shroud with the impression of Christ's crucified body which the House of Savoy has possessed since the middle of the 15th century and which was transferred from Chambéry to Turin in 1578. Panelled in dark marble with gloomy metal friezes, decorated with motifs intersecting one another in obsessive rhythms, the chapel has the disturbing atmosphere of a mausoleum, but it is surrounded by a densely fretted dome supported on small diminishing arches, each of which rests boldly on the keystone of two arches beneath it till they meet in the radiant central star against the light, the culmination of the close luminous texture.

Outside, Guarini's cupola, seen here with the unpretentious little dome of the Cathedral projected against it, is concave rather than convex in shape, and rises like a thickly fretted spire with the exotic outline of an oriental pagoda behind the unobtrusive buildings from which it emerges.

opposite page:

The Science Academy building, whose vast, severe bulk was designed by Guarini and begun in 1679, today houses some of the most important of the city's museums. Originally intended to receive the « College of Nobles » of the Society of Jesus, the edifice expresses with its compactness and regularity the austere power and uncompromising discipline of the religious order which commissioned it.

left:

Palazzo Barolo in Via delle Orfane, begun by an unknown architect in 1622 but completed by Baroncelli in 1692 for Ottavio Provana, Count of Druent. It later passed to the Falletti di Barolo family and Silvio Pellico lived in it from 1838 on.

above:

Palazzo Provana di Collegno, later Cavalchini-Garofoli, in Via S. Teresa, erected in 1698 perhaps to designs left by Guarini. The portal and balcony were altered in 1856.

opposite page:

The atrium with twisted columns and depressed vaults of Palazzo Asinari di S. Marzano (today Turati) in Via Maria Vittoria, designed in 1684 by the Ticinese Michelangelo Garove (1650-1713), but probably reflecting Guarini's ideas.

above:

The atrium, courtyard and loggia of Palazzo Paesana (Via della Consolata), the largest and most sumptuous of the private palaces in Turin, built between 1715 and 1722 by Giovan Giacomo Plantery for Baldassare Paesana di Saluzzo, knight of the Annunziata order.

left:

Atrium and courtyard of Palazzo Benso di Cavour (Via Lagrange) also built by Plantery around 1730. While not insensible to Juvarra's example, Plantery gives the Turinese baroque a more measured and solemn character, decidedly of the 18th century.

plate opposite:

The Hunting Lodge of Stupinigi, designed by Filippo Juvarra in 1729, a perfect masterpiece of late non-religious baroque. Frescoes, decorations, furniture and furnishings make it a unique document of private princely residences of the early 18th century, and it is quite exceptional for the inspiration and uniformity of its style.

Filippo Juvarra, the great architect from Messina, carried on his inspired and highly creative activity in Turin between 1714 and 1735. His experience as a scene-painter lives on in the magnificent façades of his buildings, conceived as backdrops for royal performances, and in the grandiose symmetry of his town-planning.
He was responsible for the projects, only partly realised, of two squares flanked by twin arcaded buildings, which were intended to form the monumental entrances to the city from north and west.

opposite page, above:
The beginning of Via Milano, formerly called « contrada d'Italia », from Piazza della Repubblica. Juvarra had imagined a grander complex, culminating in an imposing « Porta

Vittoria », which would commemorate the military success of 1706 and welcome travellers coming from Vercelli, Novara and Milan with regal dignity. The present buildings date from the years 1729-1731.

below:
The third enlargement of the city area was started in 1714, to the west of the old Roman castrum, in the shelter of the bastions erected at the time of the siege. This new quarter, too, had a chessboard pattern and a central square (the present Piazza Savoia). At its exit towards Porta Susina and the road to France, Juvarra erected, between 1716 and 1728, the imposing pile of the military Headquarters, characterised by the heavy pilasters and prominent relief of the cornices, thus achieving a

severely impressive effect in spite of the use of humble, unplastered brick.

following pages:
An autumnal vision of the romantic Valentino.

A glimpse of the façade of Palazzo Birago de Borgaro (later Della Valle) in Via Carlo Alberto, one of Juvarra's Turinese constructions, designed in 1715.

The vast luminous nave of the church of the Carmine, designed by Juvarra in 1732. The high side niches, the chapels closed by open arches with sinuous copings, the variety of curvilinear motifs, the elegance of the plasterwork and the whole atmosphere of radiant light make this edifice one of the masterpieces of the Messinese architect.

above:

Aerial view of the ancient centre.
The long, straight transverse
axis is Via Garibaldi, once
Via Doragrossa. The straightening was
begun in 1739 under the direction of
Giovan Giacomo Plantery and
Ignazio Bertola, thus permanently
including the medieval nucleus of the
town in its recent, grandiose
baroque extensions.

left:

The belfry added by Juvarra
(1720-1722) to the 15th century
campanile of the Cathedral; the
terminal feature was not carried out.

opposite page:

The façade of Palazzo Madama, Filippo
Juvarra's dramatic creation
(1718-1721), conceals the Roman-
medieval towers of the ancient
fortress. In this way the palace took
on its composite character,
synthesising the city's history.

preceding page:

The grand staircase of Palazzo Madama, one of the greatest masterpieces of 18th century architecture in its wonderful balance of power and grace, structure and decoration. Majestic and refined at the same time, the huge space is flooded with the light that pours in from the tall windows of the façade, which are in fact so spacious as to create effects of almost complete transparency.

above:

The complex pattern of the vaults of the central saloon of the Hunting Lodge at Stupinigi, glowing with stucco-work and frescoes.

right:

The Lodge seen through the graceful entrance gate.

Interior of the church of S. Filippo Neri (Via Maria Vittoria). The vast building, started in 1675 and entrusted to Guarini in 1697, went ahead slowly and in 1714 suffered a catastrophic fall of the dome and the front part of the nave. Reconstruction was later carried out in various stages on the basis of numerous designs elaborated by Juvarra between 1715 and 1730. The great high altar with its twisted columns, which was finished in 1703, is by Antonio Bertola.

plate opposite:

The Basilica of Superga, on the hill of the same name (2,200 ft) which dominates the city, was designed by Filippo Juvarra in 1717 and completed in 1731. In the background are the eastern slopes of the Turinese hills. The church was erected in fulfilment of a vow by Victor Amadeus II on the eve of the victorious battle of 7 September 1706 which delivered Turin from the French siege.

above:

The scenographic façade of Palazzo
Roero di Guarene (later Ferrero
d'Ormea) in Piazza Carlina, designed
by Juvarra in 1730 to add tone to an
existing group of buildings, was
started in 1685 for Giulio Chichiastro
of Chieri, Madama Reale's jeweller.
The encaustic figures which decorated
the spaces between the windows have
almost disappeared and the whole
building awaits extensive restoration.

side:

The entrance to Palazzo Martini di
Cigala (Via della Consolata) designed
by Juvarra in 1716.

103

Portal of Palazzo Isnardi di Caraglio (later Solaro del Borgo) in Piazza San Carlo, seat since 1839 of the Philharmonic Academy. The building, which preserves splendid 18th century decorations in its interior, was built in 1640 by Carlo di Castellamonte for the Marquis Havard de Senantes and was enlarged a century later by Benedetto Alfieri.

Portal of Palazzo d'Azeglio in Via Principe Amedeo. Erected in 1683 to the designs of Garove for the

Marquis Giuseppe de Marolles, the dignified residence was enlarged and decorated with very beautiful stucco-work between 1777 and 1781 by Filippo Castelli. Massimo d'Azeglio was born here on 24 October 1798.

opposite page:

Simone Martinez's fountain with Nereids and Tritons set up about 1750 in the gardens of the Royal Palace, which had been designed in 1697 by the celebrated André Le Nôtre.

Courtyard of the University (Via Po).
The building, commissioned by
Victor Amadeus II, who was preparing
a general reform of higher studies in
his dominions, was designed by Garove
in 1713 and constructed under the
direction of Giovanni Antonio Ricca,
with contributions by Bertola and
Juvarra. The general « Studio » of
Turin, which was instituted in 1403,
after peregrinations to Chieri,
Savigliano and Mondovì, found a
permanent home in Turin in 1566.
The new « Constitutions » were
enacted by the King in 1729.
Under the arcades plaques and statues
commemorate former professors who
have shed lustre on the University
throughout the centuries.

opposite page:

The compact mass, split up into
horizontal divisions which accentuate
its heaviness, of the Artillery Arsenal,
designed in 1748 by the military
engineer Antonio Felice Devincenti.
Since 1659 the site had been occupied
by the ducal « Cannon Foundry ».
Its vast extent, the lack of
openings and the severe architecture
combine to inspire a sense
of restrained power. The two allegorical
statues are a regrettable addition
of 1890, when it was decided to adorn
the building (according to the original
plans) with a monumental entrance.

The enormous Piazza Vittorio Veneto, facing the Po and the backdrop of the hills, was girt with sober neo-classical buildings in the third decade of the 19th century to designs (1818) of Giuseppe Frizzi. The « stone bridge » constructed on Napoleon's orders between 1810 and 1814, links it with the right bank of the river, on which rises the church of the Great Mother of God, a frigid imitation of the Roman Pantheon, erected by Ferdinando Bonsignore between 1818 and 1831 to express the city's thanks for its regained liberty and the return of the monarchy.

preceding page:
The square seen from the steps of the church.

A quiet corner at the opposite end of the esplanade, near the beginning of Via Po.

109

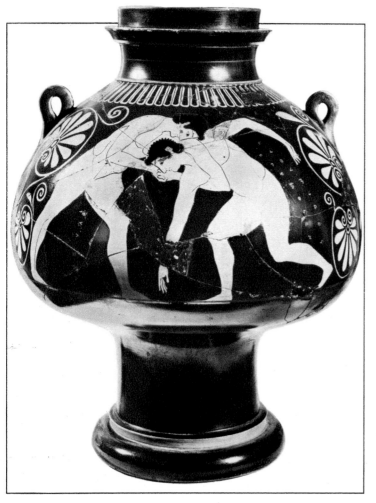

MUSEUM OF ANTIQUITIES (Science Academy Building).

page 110, above left:
Cooling vessel (« psykter ») for water or wine, signed by Eutimides. Attic pottery with black base of archaic severity (about 500 B. C.).

above right:
Armoured warrior holding a youth dressed in tunic and mantle by the arm. Bas-relief of provincial Roman art of the 1st century A. D.

below left:
Bronze helmet of pre-Roman era.

below right:
Veiled dancer. Decorative bas-relief of the end of the 1st or beginning of the 2nd century A. D. from the excavations at Industria.

The first collection of Piedmontese antiquities was begun about 1570 by Emmanuel Philibert, but the history of the Museum starts in 1723 when the Veronese scholar Scipione Maffei was first entrusted with the task of ordering inscriptions and sculptures of the Roman era. In 1832 the scattered collections were assembled in their present home, where they were gradually enriched through large acquisitions of prehistoric remains, Etruscan and Cypriot artefacts, Greek and Italic ceramics, inscriptions, statues, bas-reliefs, mosaics, bronzes, terracottas, glassware, coins, gold and silverware (the famous « Marengo treasure ») and barbarian furnishings.

EGYPTIAN MUSEUM (Science Academy Building)

in the plate, above:
Antelopes feeding. Four bearers, with the help of a donkey, carry grain to the store.
(Wall painting of tomb. About 2000 B. C.).

below:
Deceased woman offering her heart to a divinity. (Funerary papyrus. About 1000 B. C.).

The Egyptian Museum of Turin is the most important in the world after that of Cairo. The collections were begun in 1760, when Vitaliano Donati, a professor at the University, succeeded in sending home some statues he had discovered at Luxor. A decisive contribution was made in 1824 with the purchase of the precious collection assembled in Egypt by the Piedmontese Bernardino Drovetti. In the first twenty years of the 20th century the collections were appreciably enriched thanks to Ernesto Schiaparelli's excavations and, later, to the finds of Giulio Farina. A very recent and sensational acquisition is the small temple of Ellesiya, cut from the living rock to save it from the waters of the Nile, which would have submerged it owing to the erection of the Aswan dam. Among the objects of outstanding historical importance are the black granite statue of Rameses II, that of Thotmes III, the Royal papyrus, the damascened Isiac table, the intact tomb of Cha and Merie, the fragments of painted linen of the fourth millenium B. C., the « lady walking », the « gold mask », the tempera wall paintings, the vases, jewels, furnishings, tools, and weapons, which document every aspect of the most ancient Mediterranean civilisation.

opposite page:
The daring stone bridge over the Dora, with its very much flattened arch, projected by engineer Carlo Bernardo Mosca in 1830. Before the use of reinforced concrete became widespread, it was considered a marvel of statics and attracted admiring visitors.

The « Balon », the characteristic « flea-market » near Porta Palazzo.

The monument to Charles Albert, by
Carlo Marochetti, was set up in the
square bearing his name in 1861. It
represents the King with drawn sword
setting off for the Lombard frontier
in the first War of Independence.
The horse quivers with repressed
impetus, but the figure of the King
appears stiff and lifeless; on the other
hand the four handsome figures of
soldiers of the Sardinian army — the
Grenadier, the Lancer (opposite page),
the Artilleryman and the Bersagliere —
are real masterpieces. At the foot of
the monument and under the adjacent
arcades a popular trade in secondhand
books is carried on.

The Royal Armoury, instituted by Charles Albert in 1833, is housed in the Gallery of the Royal Palace erected by Benedetto Alfieri and frescoed by Claudio Francesco Beaumont in the middle of the 18th century. The collection is among the most important in Europe, being rich in complete sets of horse armour and precious weapons, both defensive and offensive, of every age and origin.

opposite page:

Two famous Turinese monuments: that, already mentioned, to Emmanuel Philibert by Carlo Marochetti (1838), and that to Ferdinand of Savoy, Duke of Genoa, by Alfonso Balzico, erected in 1877 in Piazza Solferino. The former represents the Duke in the act of sheathing his sword after the victory of St. Quentin (1557) to devote himself to the peaceful government of his dominions. The latter commemorates an episode in the battle of the Bicocca (1849), when the Prince had his horse killed under him by Austrian fire.

The cold architecture of the Restoration: the neo-classical style, imposed on public buildings by a rigid and uninspired administration, takes on funereal and prison-like tones.

above left:

The façade of the Law Courts (formerly the « Senate ») in Via Corte d'Appello: inspired by designs of Alfieri (1741), the project was completed by Ignazio Michela only in 1838.

above right:

One of the narrow, straight streets in the oldest part of the town.

right:

The military hospital of S. Luigi in Via S. Chiara, a gloomy building by Giuseppe Maria Talucchi begun in 1818. Today it houses some sections of the State Archives.

The façade of the church of S. Filippo (see p. 100), completed by Giuseppe Maria Talucchi after 1823, shows the freezing of Juvarra's imaginative ideas in the scholastic models of neo-classicism. In the background rises the block of the Academy of Sciences building by Guarino Guarini.

The church of S. Michele, built
by Pietro Bonvicini between 1784 and
1791 for the Barefooted Trinitarian
Fathers for the Ransoming of Slaves,
and the adjoining monastery which
overlooks the gardens of Piazza
Cavour. The undulating ground of
this island of green is all that remains
of the spacious gardens of the Ripari,
which were created after the
Restoration on the site of the ramparts
of the fortifications pulled down
during the French occupation.

left:

The characteristic public fountain,
of cast iron painted green, which
pours out its clear water from the
nostrils of a meek-looking young bull.
Hence the popular name of « 'l toret ».

CIVIC MUSEUM OF ANCIENT ART (Palazzo Madama).

plate on preceding page:

Antonello da Messina. Portrait of an Unknown Man (1476).

This is one of the unchallenged masterpieces of fifteenth century portraiture and of the painting of all time: a moment of supreme balance between the penetrating analysis of the Flemings and the monumental synthesis of Giotto and Masaccio. The unknown sitter, in his close-fitting red jacket fluted like the shaft of a Doric column, his shoulder shaded by a band of his black cap, looks at us with the impassive, but covertly aggressive self-assurance of a mafioso. **A hint of distrust in the eye, a veil of irony on the lips combine to trace a disquieting psychological portrait with exemplary economy of expression.**

The Civic Museum of Ancient Art started in 1863 as the Museum of Industrial Design and it is to this origin that it owes its splendid collections, which have gradually been added to, of mosaics, wooden sculptures and carvings, painted and inlaid furniture, stained glass, gold and coloured glassware, Gothic and baroque wrought iron, weapons, musical instruments, ivories, leather work, majolica, porcelain, materials, lacework, embroidery, goldware, jewels, silverware, pewter, bronzes, enamels, coins (over a hundred thousand), drawings, prints, bindings, ex libris, sedan chairs, carriages and boats. To these we may add the ethnographic collections of pre-Columbian America, archaeological and art collections of the Middle and Far East, the 28 superb pages of the masterpiece of 15th century illuminated work (*Les très belles heures du Duc de Berry*), the Missal of Cardinal Della Rovere illuminated by Giovanni da Parma, the Madonna and Child of Tino da Camaino, panels and canvases by Giacomo Jacquerio, Martino Spanzotti, Defendente Ferrari, Tanzio da Varallo, Pontormo, Tiepolo and many others. A museum in itself is represented by the exquisite series of 17th and 18th century rooms of Madama Reale's apartments, which house part of the collections.

Another typically bureaucratic building
of bare severity and efficiency: the
Poor-house, constructed in 1888 to the
designs of Crecentino Caselli, along the
straight road leading to Stupinigi.

right:

The monument to Giuseppe Garibaldi
in Corso Cairoli. Designed by Odoardo
Tabacchi (1887), it is typically
Subalpine in the unpretentiousness
of its proportions and its restrained
realism.

The Gallery of Subalpine Industry, which joins Piazza Castello and Piazza Carlo Alberto, is a singular example of « belle époque » taste (1874), in the heart of the old city. It was designed by Pietro Carrera.

below:

The very lively food market of Porta Palazzo (Piazza della Repubblica).

The axis of the extremely long Corso Regina Margherita, the great artery running north of the historic centre, with Piazza della Repubblica and the popular market of Porta Palazzo (1814). The small arcaded square to the right was designed by Filippo Juvarra in 1731 as an approach to the city from Milan. Higher up on the right may be seen the monumental complex of the Palatine Towers, the Royal Palace and the Cathedral; in the background the ever present spire of the Mole Antonelliana. On the left the last bends of the Dora wind in and out. The oblique thoroughfare to the right, which skirts the Royal Gardens, is Corso S. Maurizio, built over the site of the old northern ramparts.

Piazza Castello, the historic centre of the city, with the composite mass of Palazzo Madama. To the left may be seen Guarini's dome of S. Lorenzo (1680), the Piazzetta Reale, the Archives building (1734) and the Royal Theatre, in course of reconstruction. The broad thoroughfare running obliquely to the right is Via Po. It has arcades on both sides and connects the square to Piazza Vittorio Veneto and the bank of the river. As the principal axis of the second enlargement of the town, the « contrada di Po » was designed in 1673 by Amedeo di Castellamonte and through its unusual width, the uniformity of its buildings and the austere dignity of its architecture immediately constituted an impressive model of functional town planning.

below:

The station of Porta Nuova, completed in 1868 to the plans of Alessandro Mazzucchetti, bears traces of the neo-gothic taste of the time. The Turin-Genoa line had been inaugurated in 1853.

The lower and working class district
of S. Salvario, laid out in 1854 to the
south of the historic centre, between
the railway to Genoa and the Po. In the
centre, the neo-Romanesque spires
of the church of the S. Cuore
di Maria, designed by Carlo Ceppi
in 1884.

Two « fin de siècle » monuments in the Valentino: the whirling, curving Fountain of the Seasons, designed by Carlo Ceppi for the National Exhibition of 1898, and the equestrian monument to Amedeo of Savoy, Duke of Aosta, boldly cast in bronze by Davide Calandra, unveiled in 1902. It represents the young Prince at the battle of Custoza checking his horse as it rears to face the charge of the Uhlans. The whole is modelled with perfect late-Romantic sensibility in which the realism of the details is fused in an almost impressionistic dynamism.

opposite page:

Turin boasts illustrious theatrical and musical traditions, only partly dimmed by changed customs and the destruction of some famous theatres like the Regio and the Rossini. The open air performances (above) held every summer in the Gardens of the Royal Palace attract a numerous

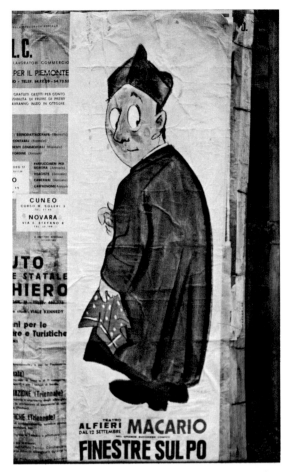

public. The vast auditorium of the Rai-TV (below) offers musical performances of a very high level: the hall represents the radical transformation (1952) of one built in 1856 for horse shows but soon after turned into an Opera House.

A popular figure of the Piedmontese dialect theatre.

below:

No longer the traditional old woman at the corner, but the « motorised » seller of roast chestnuts.

Antonio del Pollaiolo,
« Tobias and the Angel » (about 1465),
one of the masterpieces of the
Sabauda Gallery.

SABAUDA GALLERY (Academy of Sciences Building).

The gallery owes its origin and name to the collections of the Dukes of Savoy, later Kings of Sardinia, who made them available to scholars and visitors in 1832 and who in 1860 presented them to the state. In 1959 the present museological arrangement, essentially functional and dignified in character, was completed. Thanks to the purchase (1741) of the notable works of art assembled in his Viennese palaces by Prince Eugene of Savoy, the Gallery contains the most significant Italian collection of masters of the Low Countries such as Jan van Eyck, Petrus Christus, Roger van der Weyden, Rembrandt, Van Dyck, Ruisdael, Gerard Dou and Paulus Potter. The crowded scenes from *The Passion of Jesus Christ* by Hans Memling, the *Old Man Sleeping* by Rembrandt, the rarefied spirituality of the *Interior of a Synagogue* by Saenredam are all obligatory stops in an unhurried visit. Great Italian painting, too, is worthily represented in the Gallery by panels and canvases of Giotto's predecessors, Fra Angelico, Pollaiolo, Mantegna, not to mention Veronese and Bronzino, Guercino, Tintoretto, Gentileschi, Tiepolo, Canaletto and Guardi. Along with these Martino Spanzotti, Defendente and Gaudenzio Ferrari, Giovenone, Macrino d'Alba and Sodoma amply document the flowering of Piedmontese painting in the late Renaissance.

CIVIC GALLERY OF MODERN ART (Via Magenta 31)

preceding plate:
Antonio Fontanesi, After the Rain (c. 1870).

The Gallery of Modern Art broke away in 1891 from the Civic Museum of Turin and in 1895 was transferred to its present site, in a pavilion provisionally erected in 1880 by Guglielmo Calderini for the National Exhibition. Partly destroyed by bombs in 1942, the edifice was rebuilt in a courageously modern style as the result of a much debated competition (1952), by the young architects Carlo Bassi and Goffredo Boschetti.
The Gallery contains almost all the masterpieces of Antonio Fontanesi, who taught at the Albertina Academy in Turin from 1869 to 1882, the year of his death. It provides an extensive documentation of all Piedmontese painting of the nineteenth and twentieth centuries from Massimo d'Azeglio to Gamba, Gastaldi, Quadrone and Reycend down to Gonin, Biscarra, Pelizza, Volpedo and Falchetti. The most sensitive pupils of Fontanesi are thus worthily represented (Calderini, Follini, Pollonera), as well as the exponents of the Canavese « Rivara school » (Pittara, Pastoris, Avondo), and the vigorous realism of Lorenzo Delleani beside the prodigious technical virtuosity of Giacomo Grosso. The other Italian Schools, too, are represented by their greatest nineteenth century masters with Hayez and Cremona, Toma and Lega, Mosè Bianchi and Antonio Mancini, Fattori and Signorini, Boldini and Ciardi, Tito and Spadini, down to the more recent Modigliani, Boccioni, Scipione, Carrà and Tosi; then from Viani, Morandi, Casorati, Spazzapan, Rosai and De Pisis to contemporary artists such as Afro, Santomaso, Cassinari, Morlotti, Guttuso and many others.
Among foreign artists works of Renoir, Courbet, Utrillo, Picasso, Chagall, Léger and Klee stand out. The section devoted to sculpture also boasts notable works by Canova, Marochetti, Vela, Calandra, Bistolfi and Medardo Rosso, down to the contemporaries Martini and Marini, Viani and Mastroianni, Messina and Manzù. With its periodical exhibitions of international repute, the great hall for frequent conferences, and the 20,000 volumes of the specialised public library, the Gallery may be considered one of the greatest institutions of artistic culture in Europe.

opposite page, above:
The immense single-span vault of the central hall (10,000 sq. m.) in the Torino-Esposizioni building, a daring and impressive work by Pier Luigi Nervi (1948).

below:
The Municipal Stadium, capable of holding 80,000 spectators, built in 1933 to the plans of engineers Bianchini, Fagnoni and Ortensi.

preceding page, above:

The Angelica Fountain in Piazza Solferino, designed by Giovanni Riva in 1930. The rhetorically bombastic figures stand out against the leafy foliage of the horse-chestnuts in Corso Re Umberto I.

below:

The original, functional edifice of the Civic Gallery of Modern Art in Via Magenta.

above:

The Palace of Labour, the imposing construction designed by Pier Luigi Nervi for the « Italia '61 » Exhibition. The huge parallelepiped, supported on 16 pillars 25 metres high, has a total volume of 650,000 cubic metres.

below:

The Automobile Museum, designed by Amedeo Albertini (1960). In the foreground the great symbolic wheel in embossed bronze of the monument to the Military Transport Driver by Renato Costa and Goffredo Verginelli (1965).

above:

The Humanistic Faculties building of the University, in Via S. Ottavio (1968). Designed by the architects F. Bardelli, S. Hutter, G. Levi Montalcini and D. Morelli, its structures of steel, aluminium and glass occupy a space of 155,000 cubic metres.

right:

The flow of immigrants with their cardboard suitcases and their burdens of ancient sufferings and new hopes who come to Turin from every part of Italy, but above all from the South, in search of a secure job and a more civilised standard of living.

opposite page:

The RAI building in Via Cernaia (72 metres high, over 110,000 cubic metres in volume). Designed by the architects Domenico Morelli and Aldo Morbelli, it was finished in 1966.

Among the fields of the suburbs the houses of the new working-class settlements stretch as far as the eye can see, monotonously but decorously aligned in regular blocks along the broad avenues. Where a few years ago corn was sown, now new districts spread out one after the other, in which even the native Turinese wanders like a stranger. The future of Turin as a « city » — not a mere agglomeration that is always becoming more populous and chaotic but a civilised place for living in — lies in its ability to infuse into this immense periphery the austere sense of discipline and hidden grace which have made its historic centre not only an admired model of urban civilisation but the expression of a way of life, a repository of affections and memories, in other words a home.